SRA
BUILDING
Vocabulary
Skills

Level 6
Student Edition

Columbus, OH • Chicago, IL • Redmond, WA

The **McGraw·Hill** Companies

www.sra4kids.com

 SRA

Send all inquiries to:
SRA/McGraw-Hill
8787 Orion Place
Columbus, OH 43240-4027

Printed in the United States of America.

ISBN 0-07-579617-1

1 2 3 4 5 6 7 8 9 QPD 07 06 05 04 03 02

The **McGraw-Hill** Companies

Table of Contents

Unit 3

Unit 4

Vocabulary List

1. **perseverance**
   (pûr´ sə vir´ əns) *n.*
   determination; sticking
   to a goal

2. **accomplishment**
   (ə kom´ plish mənt) *n.*
   achievement

3. **ordeal**
   (or dēl´) *n.*
   painful experience

4. **unpredictable**
   (un´ pri dik´ tə bəl) *adj.*
   not certain

5. **optimism**
   (op´ tə miz´ əm) *n.*
   hopefulness

6. **critic**
   (krit´ ik) *n.*
   a faultfinder

7. **endeavor**
   (en dev´ ər) *n.*
   try

8. **rigorous**
   (rig´ ər əs) *adj.*
   harsh

9. **valiant**
   (val´ yənt) *adj.*
   brave

10. **ingenious**
    (in jēn´ yəs) *adj.*
    clever

"Perseverance" Vocabulary

1 Word Meanings

Clarifying for Meaning

Circle the definition of each boldfaced word in the sentences below.

1. The Wright brothers encountered more than one **critic,** or faultfinder, who did not believe that their airplane would fly.

2. Landing on the moon was a huge **accomplishment**—an achievement that will never be forgotten.

3. Amelia Earhart made an **endeavor,** or attempt, to fly around the world, but she was never seen again.

4. As a result of his **valiant,** or brave, efforts, Charles Lindbergh won the flight competition.

5. Air Force pilots go through training that is **rigorous,** or severe and punishing.

6. Astronauts look at their missions with **optimism**—a strong belief that everything will turn out for the best.

7. In the 1960s, U. S. scientists had to be **ingenious**—clever—to figure out how to send humans to the moon.

8. Getting used to Earth's gravity after being in space is a big **ordeal.** This painful experience involves rebuilding muscle tissue lost during a long period of weightlessness.

9. Through **perseverance**—persistence—the United States was the first country to put a person on the moon.

10. Many pilots won't fly when the weather is **unpredictable,** or uncertain.

2 Reference Skills

Connotation

  Use a dictionary to look up each pair of synonyms. Study their definitions and example sentences. Then put a check mark next to the word that has the more positive connotation. If one word does not have a more positive connotation that the other, leave both squares blank.

1. accomplishment ☐ act ☐

2. ordeal ☐ test ☐

3. unpredictable ☐ volatile ☐

4. valiant ☐ bold ☐

5. endeavor ☐ struggle ☐

6. rigorous ☐ difficult ☐

  Underline the word from the pair in parentheses that best fits each sentence, based on its connotation. If you need to, look up the words in the dictionary.

7. Ever since she was a little girl, her highest *(aspiration/goal)* has been to become a doctor.

8. The *(valiant/bold)* soldiers won the war and returned home unharmed.

9. Navigating the ship in hurricane weather was the worst *(ordeal/test)* the captain had ever been through.

10. Most people could not complete the *(hard/rigorous)* training required of a Navy Seal.

  Think About It

When trying to determine which word has a more positive connotation, remember books or movies that you have read or seen that use either word. This will give you a visual picture of the word.

Vocabulary List

1. perseverance

2. accomplishment

3. ordeal

4. unpredictable

5. optimism

6. critic

7. endeavor

8. rigorous

9. valiant

10. ingenious

③ Build New Vocabulary

Noun and Verb Forms

 Divide each noun into both its verb form and its suffix and write the verb form and suffix in the blank.

1. perseverance _____

2. accomplishment _____

3. optimism _____

•••

Read each sentence. Fill in the blank with the noun or verb from above that best fits the sentence.

4. During the Dust Bowl years, many farmers found it hard to

_____.

5. The carmaker decided to _____ the new model's gas mileage to make it more appealing to low-income families.

6. It was a great _____ for peacemakers to tear down the Berlin Wall.

7. The doctor's _____ helped her patient feel more comfortable about the surgery.

8. Even though he fell many times, the ice-skater's

_____ helped him land the jump.

9. The federal employees _____ a great deal of work on roads and bridges.

10. The teacher wanted to _____ the time that the students spent on the field trip.

11. Ireland was able to _____ after the Potato Famine.

12. The completion of the Chunnel, the underwater tunnel between

England and France, is one of the greatest _____ of the late twentieth century.

 **Word Play**

Informal Language

Study the informal language that is used to define each vocabulary word. Then fill in each blank with the informal word or phrase that best completes the sentence.

Vocabulary Words	Informal Language
endeavor	to take a shot at
perseverance	stick-to-it-tiveness
optimism	looking at the world through rose-colored glasses
rigorous	no picnic
ordeal	hassle
critics	nitpickers
unpredictable	iffy
valiant	gutsy
accomplishment	done deal
ingenious	cool

1. One day, Thomas Edison came up with a _____ idea.

2. He wanted _____ inventing a lightbulb.

3. Finding the right material to put in the lightbulb was a real

_____.

4. _____ said his idea would never work.

5. By 1879, he had perfected his lightbulb—it was a

_____.

6. Through his _____, Edison produced more than 1,000 patents!

7. He had a way of _____ because he believed he would eventually succeed.

8. It was _____ doing experiment after experiment on his lightbulb.

9. The outcomes of many of his experiments were very

_____.

10. All in all, Edison's dedication and hard work proved that he was one

_____ guy.

Vocabulary for "Hard Times"

1. **reformer**
   (ri form´ ər) *n.*
   one who urges
   improvement

2. **destitute**
   (des´ ti tōōt´) *adj.*
   very poor

3. **solitary**
   (sol´ i ter´ ē) *adj.*
   being alone

4. **cramped**
   (krampt) *adj.*
   crowded

5. **crisis**
   (krī´ sis) *n.*
   difficult time

6. **deprive**
   (di prīv´) *v.*
   to take away

7. **stranded**
   (stran´ ded) *adj.*
   left in a helpless place

8. **afflicted**
   (ə flik´ tid) *adj.*
   in pain or suffering

9. **salvation**
   (sal vā´ shən) *n.*
   a saving; rescue

10. **devastation**
    (dev´ ə stā´ shən) *n.*
    destruction

1 Word Meanings

Definitions

Write the letter of the correct definition next to each vocabulary word.

1. ___ crisis

2. ___ stranded

3. ___ cramped

4. ___ devastation

5. ___ solitary

6. ___ destitute

7. ___ reformer

8. ___ afflicted

9. ___ salvation

10. ___ deprive

A. the act of saving or the condition of being saved from something; redemption

B. being, traveling, or living without others; alone; unaccompanied

C. lacking room or space, as for movement or placement

D. a person who works to bring about improvement

E. the act or instance of destroying or ruining, or the destruction or ruin thus caused

F. an unstable or uncertain situation, as in international relations, that has the potential for sudden change

G. to take a possession or attribute away from

H. having no money or other means of living

I. experiencing physical or mental suffering

J. left in a helpless or difficult position

Think About It

If you are having a hard time matching a vocabulary word to its definition, try looking for these clues: 1) If a definition has the word *person* in it, see whether you have any words on your list that end in *-er, -or,* or *-ist* because these are some common endings of words for people. 2) If a definition starts with the word *to,* then you have a big clue that the definition probably belongs to a verb.

② Reference Skills

Word Choice

 Study the thesaurus entries and shortened dictionary entries below. Complete each sentence by writing the dictionary word that best fits.

> **Thesaurus**
> salvation *n.* liberation, rescue, safekeeping
>
> **Dictionary**
> liberation *n.* **1.** the setting free of; release: *liberating slaves*
> rescue *n.* **1.** the saving or freeing of, as from danger: *the rescue of the hostages*
> safekeeping *n.* **1.** protection or care: *to leave a necklace in the safekeeping of a grandparent*

1. Risking his own life, John F. Kennedy made a daring

   _____ of a wounded crew member after his

   boat was sliced in two.

2. Early feminists sought the _____ of women
   from their economic dependence on men.

3. Before going to war, the soldier gave his grandfather's watch to his

   wife for _____.

> **Thesaurus**
> cramped *adj.* narrow, snug, tight
>
> **Dictionary**
> narrow *adj.* **1.** having little width; not broad: *a narrow stream*
> snug *adj.* **1.** comfortable and warm; cozy: *a snug bed*
> tight *adj.* **1.** fastened or held firmly: *a tight lid*

4. There was not enough room for two cars on the

   _____ bridge.

5. On their camping trip, the Smith family slept in a

   _____ cabin in the woods.

6. We wanted to cool off the room, but the window was too

   _____ to open.

Vocabulary List

1. reformer
2. destitute
3. solitary
4. cramped
5. crisis
6. deprive
7. stranded
8. afflicted
9. salvation
10. devastation

③ Build New Vocabulary

Context Clues

Write the vocabulary word that fits best in each sentence, based on general context clues.

1. After being lost in the desert, the men stumbled upon a spring. Rejoicing, they drank the lifesaving water. The spring was their

   _____.

2. After being injured in a soccer game, Jim was

   _____ with a pulled muscle in his leg. He could not play for three weeks.

3. Mika decided to take a shortcut to the park. When she had walked several blocks without recognizing anything, she found herself

   _____.

4. Isabella looked sadly out the window as her roommates left for the

   movies. She would have to spend a _____ evening in the apartment.

5. Mr. Peréz packed the car for the trip to Florida. Even though he warned his children that they would have to sit close together, they

   still complained that they were _____.

6. Dr. Martin Luther King, Jr. fought for equal rights, and people listened to what he had to say about improving the lives of

   African Americans. He was a great social _____.

7. Ling did not learn English before she visited England. She had a

   _____ because she could not understand anyone.

8. The volcano erupted, and lava covered the city. All the townspeople survived, but they lost their homes. No one escaped the

   _____.

 **4** Word Play

Crossword Puzzle

 Complete the crossword puzzle below using the vocabulary words.

Across

2. in pain
3. no one else is there
6. destruction
9. having no money
10. too many people in a room

Down

1. rescue
4. hard time
5. someone who wants change
7. on a desert island
8. to take away

1. **sullen**
   (sul´ ən) *adj.*
   silent and gloomy

2. **reluctant**
   (ri luk´ tənt) *adj.*
   unwilling

3. **dignified**
   (dig´ nə fīd´) *adj.*
   important looking

4. **triumphant**
   (trī um´ fənt) *adj.*
   successful

5. **pretentious**
   (pri ten´ shəs) *adj.*
   showing off

6. **jovial**
   (jō´ vē əl) *adj.*
   merry; jolly

7. **cynical**
   (sin´ i kəl) *adj.*
   always doubting

8. **lanky**
   (lang´ kē) *adj.*
   long and thin

9. **diminutive**
   (di min´ yə tiv) *adj.*
   very small

10. **unkempt**
    (un kempt´) *adj.*
    not neat in appearance

Describing People

1 Word Meanings

Synonyms

 Write the vocabulary word that fits each set of synonyms. Look up the synonyms in the dictionary if necessary.

1. opposed, hesitation, resistant _____

2. ragged, untidy, sloppy _____

3. glum, sulky, gloomy _____

4. puny, miniature, little _____

5. festive, lively, cheerful _____

6. victorious, prosperous, effective _____

7. sarcastic, scornful, bitter _____

8 noble, stately, honorable _____

9. self-important, showy, arrogant, _____

10. slender, lean, skinny _____

2 Reference Skills

Antonyms

Read each vocabulary word and its antonym listed in the box below. Look up and study each antonym in a thesaurus. Then complete each sentence by writing the antonym that best fits.

sullen, chipper	dignified, ashamed	reluctant, eager
triumphant, unsuccessful	pretentious, modest	cynical, respectful
diminutive, great	jovial, gloomy	

1. The crew of the space shuttle *Challenger* was excited and

   _____ to begin the mission.

2. Aboard the *Challenger* was a high school teacher named Christa McAuliffe. Her students and fellow teachers liked her because she

   was _____ of others.

3. Being the _____ person she was, Christa McAuliffe accepted the offer, which pleased everyone at her school.

4. Her students became _____ when the *Challenger* blew apart.

5. Christa McAuliffe had a _____ spirit and always looked at the bright side of things.

6. Even if were raining outside, Christa McAuliffe's

   _____ personality brightened any classroom.

7. Although the *Challenger* mission was _____, the crew will always be remembered.

8. Christa McAuliffe's students and peers will never be

   _____ to say that she was their friend.

Vocabulary List

1. sullen
2. reluctant
3. dignified
4. triumphant
5. pretentious
6. jovial
7. cynical
8. lanky
9. diminutive
10. unkempt

3 Build New Vocabulary

Context Clues

Write the vocabulary word that fits best in each sentence, based on general context clues. Look up unfamiliar words in a dictionary.

1. During medieval times, _____ kings and queens invited jesters into their courts.

2. Jesters were _____ characters who juggled, played instruments, and performed slapstick in hopes of making the king or queen happy.

3. Jesters often looked _____ because they patched together loose bits of cloth to make something warm to wear.

4. Mostly men were court jesters, and they came in a variety shapes and sizes, from _____ to

   _____.

5. Sometimes jesters were _____ to visit the king or queen because they did not want to be punished for a poor performance.

6. _____ kings and queens would not invite a jester to court because he belonged to a lower social class.

7. However, _____ kings and queens rewarded jesters for a job well done.

• •

Complete the passage below using the remaining vocabulary words.

Sid, the _____ jester, sat on the stairs and sulked because he was sure his song had displeased Sir Sebastion. But Trevor, the

Transylvanian jester, knew he was _____ because he had tickled him with a tulip while he played his trumpet.

4 Word Play

Dialogue in a Play

Read the lines and stage directions from the play below. Then write the vocabulary word that makes the most sense in each blank. Refer to stage directions for clues.

(Enter Benedick and others on horseback; all laughing)

BEATRICE: *(approaching Benedick)* Why are you looking so

_____, Benedick? Did you trick someone into believing you are an honest man?

BENEDICK: *(climbing off the horse)* Where are your manners, Beatrice? Is it no longer the custom to say hello with a smile?

BEATRICE: I do not know why I bother talking to you. Your tongue is

sharp, and you look _____.

BENEDICK: *(with a smile on his face)* I prefer being called quick-witted, yet I agree with you that my appearance is a little ragged. But as you know, I have been abroad for some time now. So I believe I have successfully explained myself, but what is your excuse for being so

_____? I believe you are distrustful of every living thing.

BEATRICE: *(walks up to Benedick and looks straight into his eyes)* I have decided to behave in this manner because I am constantly surrounded by

_____ people who claim to be more important than they really are.

BENEDICK: Or maybe you are just _____ to let people get close to you and acquaint themselves with the real you.

BEATRICE: *(turning away from Benedick)* Benedick, you should not talk about things you cannot possibly understand. I have wasted enough time speaking with you. Good-bye.

BENEDICK: *(waving to Beatrice)* Good-bye, Beatrice. It was wonderful chatting with you. *(lowering his voice)* I believe we both know who was

_____ in this quick exchange of words!

Vocabulary List

1. **wrath**
   (rath) *n.*
   extreme anger

2. **severe**
   (sə vir´) *adj.*
   strict; harsh

3. **scoundrel**
   (skoun´ drəl) *n.*
   evil, dishonest person

4. **vandalism**
   (van´ də liz´ əm) *n.*
   unlawful destruction

5. **menace**
   (men´ is) *n.*
   a threat

6. **venomous**
   (ven´ ə məs) *adj.*
   poisonous

7. **banish**
   (ban´ ish) *v.*
   to force to leave

8. **corrupt**
   (kə rupt´) *v.*
   to cause to act badly;
   make rotten

9. **malignant**
   (mə lig´ nənt) *adj.*
   evil; harmful

10. **scowl**
    (skoul) *v.*
    to frown angrily

Vocabulary for Villains

 **Word Meanings**

Association

 Write the vocabulary word that fits best in each sentence.

1. The cobra is a _____ snake that injects a deadly poison into its victims.

2. Hank Ketcham wrote a comic strip, called "Dennis the _____," about a mischievious boy whose behavior constantly disrupts his neighbor's quiet home.

3. A _____ thunderstorm is one that is harsher and causes more destruction than other storms.

4. In *Romeo and Juliet*, officials _____ Romeo from the city for killing Juliet's cousin.

5. The Grinch, a grumpy, mean character created by Dr. Seuss, always has a _____ on his face.

6. In the Middle Ages, _____ knights would try to take over kingdoms.

7. Pouring toxic chemicals into a lake will _____ the water supply.

8. Although he is sometimes glorified in western movies, Jesse James was a _____ and a criminal.

9. A child who behaves poorly at school will have to face the _____ of an unhappy parent.

10. Alarm systems help protect people's homes from _____, such as theft and property destruction.

2 Reference Skills

Reference Tools

 Read each sentence. Then answer the question that follows to indicate which reference tool listed below will help you locate the information that you need.

Reference Tools: dictionary, rhyming dictionary, thesaurus, book of quotations

---

1. The scoundrel ran off with the old woman's purse.
   Where would you find the definition of *scoundrel?*

   _____

2. Robert received a severe punishment when he forgot to pick up his little sister from school.
   Where would you find a synonym for *severe?*

   _____

3. The wrath of King Kong was evident when he climbed the Empire State Building.
   Where would you find a word that rhymes with *wrath?*

   _____

4. Mary Queen of Scots was a menace to the throne of Queen Elizabeth I.
   Where could you find a quote by Queen Elizabeth I?

   _____

5. Toilet-papering someone's house is an act of vandalism.
   Where could you find an example sentence that includes the word *vandalism?*

   _____

6. The teacher had a scowl on her face when the student told her that his dog ate his homework.
   Where can you locate an antonym for *scowl?*

   _____

Vocabulary List

1. *wrath*

2. *severe*

3. *scoundrel*

4. *vandalism*

5. *menace*

6. *venomous*

7. *banish*

8. *corrupt*

9. *malignant*

10. *scowl*

3 Build New Vocabulary

Word Parts

The following words contain the word part *mal*. Examine the meaning of each word's other part and draw a line to its definition.

> *mal*: from *malus*, Latin for "bad"

Definition

1. malaria: *mal* + *aria*, Italian for "air"

2. malodorous: *mal* + *odorus*, Latin for "smelling"

3. malcontent: *mal* + *content*, Latin for "happy"

4. malfunction: *mal* + *function*, Latin for "perform"

5. malignant: *mal* + *gignere*, Latin for "bring about"

A. bad smelling

B. perform badly

C. bad or infected air

D. bringing about of something bad

E. not happy; dissatisfied

Write the word from the list above that best completes each sentence below.

6. _____ is an illness that people once thought was caused by infected air.

7. Epilepsy is caused by a _____ of the brain.

8. Because of negative side effects, many doctors are

_____ with some of the medicines used for epilepsy.

9. Severe wounds that are left untreated can become

_____ because of the gas that they give off.

10. If it is noticed early enough, a _____ tumor can be removed.

4 Word Play

Rhymes

 Some of the vocabulary words have different forms and can be used as different parts of speech. Keeping this in mind, write the vocabulary word or a form of it that best completes each rhyme.

1. As he stomped angrily down the path, one could say he was full of _____.

2. Every time the neighbor's dog started howling, the man covered his ears and began _____.

3. Although my grandma is very dear, she can also be quite _____.

4. You don't want to play tennis with Dennis, for I hear he is quite a _____.

5. The king decided that he would _____ someone he wished would simply vanish.

6. There was a big scandal because no one could find the _____.

7. It was not nice for the visitor to disrupt and _____ the class.

8. How could someone who seems so benign, slander, injure, and _____?

1. apathy
(ap′ ə thē) *n.*
lack of feeling

2. indignation
(in′ dig nā′ shən) *n.*
anger

3. conscientious
(kon′ shē en′ shəs) *adj.*
careful

4. superstitious
(sōō′ pər stish′ əs) *adj.*
having unreasonable beliefs

5. dismayed
(dis mād′) *adj.*
alarmed

6. morale
(mə ral′) *n.*
attitude or spirit

7. humiliation
(hū mil′ ē a′ shən) *n.*
shame

8. intuition
(in′ tōō ish′ ən) *n.*
a hunch

9. contemplation
(kon′ təm plā′ shən) *n.*
deep thought

10. skeptical
(skep′ ti kəl) *adj.*
doubtful

"It's All in Your Head"

1 Word Meanings

Prior Knowledge

 Read each situation described below. Then write the vocabulary word that best fits the situation.

1. You see an ad on TV for a product that supposedly melts fat away while you sleep. Because you doubt that this is true, you are very

   _____.

2. You are ice-skating, performing a routine for a panel of judges. As you proudly show off your jumps, you fall several times during your routine.

   You feel _____.

3. For no logical reason at all, you suddenly feel the need to call home.

   Your _____ tells you to do it.

4. Your team has just lost five games in a row. Even the coach is hanging his

   head. The _____ of the team is at an all-time low.

5. Your dentist is always careful to cause you as little pain as possible. She asks how you feel, adjusts pain medication if necessary, and in

   general is very _____.

6. Your grandmother broke a mirror. Being very

   _____, she is now convinced that she will have seven years of bad luck.

7. You are taking a test and are so deep in _____ that you don't even hear the bell ring.

8. A store detective is convinced that you shoplifted something and demands that you empty your pockets. You are innocent, so you feel

   a rising sense of _____.

9. You read the paper and are _____ at all the bad news that is being reported.

10. Your brother uses your things after you have told him over and over again how much it upsets you. He doesn't seem to care. His complete

    _____ makes you even angrier.

2 Reference Skills

Syllabication

The vocabulary words below are divided into syllables for hyphenation. Following each one is the beginning of a line of text. At the end of each line are spaces that show how many letter spaces are left for the vocabulary word. Based on the number of letter spaces left on the line, figure out the best place to hyphenate the word and write it on the spaces. Remember to count the hyphen as one letter space.

1. (ap • a • thy) The voters showed their __ __ __ __ __

   _____

2. (in • dig • na • tion) The new senator felt __ __ __ __ __ __

   _____

3. (con • sci • en • tious) The mail carrier won an award for being

   __ __ __ __ __ __ __ __ __ __   _____

4. (su • per • sti • tious) Even today, many people are

   __ __ __ __ __ __ __   _____

5. (dis • mayed) The firefighters rushed out of the building, __ __ __ __

   _____

6. (mo • rale) Officials tried to boost __ __ __ __ __

   _____

7. (hu • mil • i • a • tion) The cheater felt great __ __ __ __ __ __ __

   _____

8. (in • tu • i • tion) Some people believe in women's __ __ __

   _____

9. (con • tem • pla • tion) The president sat in deep

   __ __ __ __ __ __ __ __   _____

10. (skep • ti • cal) Investors were __ __ __ __ __ __

    _____

Vocabulary List

1. *apathy*

2. *indignation*

3. *conscientious*

4. *superstitious*

5. *dismayed*

6. *morale*

7. *humiliation*

8. *intuition*

9. *contemplation*

10. *skeptical*

 3 Build New Vocabulary

Adverb Forms

 Change the vocabulary words below into adverbs by adding the suffix *–ly*.

1. conscientious _____

2. superstitious _____

3. skeptical _____

 Complete each sentence using the newly formed adverb from above that fits best.

4. The police officer stopped Gretchen for speeding and asked to see her driver's license. After she handed it to him, the officer looked at her license

_____ because Gretchen did not look like the picture on her license.

5. Paco wanted to go outside and play football with his friends, but

instead he stayed inside and worked _____ on his book report.

6. Kimyata looked at his watch _____. The clock had struck noon and he was afraid that if he did not eat something, he would disappear.

 Complete each sentence using the vocabulary word from the first part of the exercise.

7. People who pick up a penny for good luck are

_____.

8. Looking both ways before crossing a busy street is being

_____.

4 Word Play

Same, Opposite, or Unrelated?

 For each pair of words, decide whether the meanings are the same, opposite, or completely unrelated. Write your answers in the blanks.

1. contemplation, reflection _____

2. dismayed, attractive _____

3. conscientious, careless _____

4. apathy, curiosity _____

5. superstitious, desirable _____

6. indignation, fury _____

7. morale, spirit _____

8. humiliation, pride _____

9. intuition, insight _____

10. skeptical, suspicious _____

Vocabulary Review

① Review Word Meanings

Read the passage below. Then answer the questions about the boldfaced vocabulary words.

Black Plague

Early in 1347, a disease attacked what is now the southern Ukraine. It was called the Bubonic Plague or Black Plague. Those who were **afflicted** with the disease suffered terribly. They experienced horrible pain and strange movements of their limbs. Four days after the first symptoms appeared, their skin blackened as a result of lung failure, and they died. The plague was seen as **malignant,** causing death in anywhere from 30 percent to 75 percent of all cases. No one knew the disease's cause, so the natives in the region turned their **wrath** on the Italian traders and blamed them for the **devastation** that it caused.

As the plague spread throughout Europe, whole groups of people would be **banished** from countries in an effort to keep the disease away. Those who showed symptoms often prayed for **salvation,** hoping to be saved from the disease. The people did not know it then, but the whole cause of the miserable **ordeal** was fleas that lived on rats. When a rat died, the fleas, carrying the deadly bubonic bacteria, would find a new host, which was often a human being. The **crisis** finally started to end in the early 1350s when, after killing nearly half of the European population, the Black Plague slowly faded away.

• •

Now read the following questions. Then completely fill in the bubble of the correct answer.

1. According to the passage, what is the definition of *wrath?*
   - Ⓐ great anger
   - Ⓑ hospitality
   - Ⓒ army

2. If someone was *afflicted* with the plague, he or she experienced _____.
   - Ⓐ peace of mind
   - Ⓑ pain and suffering
   - Ⓒ a great talent

3. What does *malignant* mean in the passage?
   - Ⓐ evil
   - Ⓑ treatable
   - Ⓒ eventually causing death

4. In this passage, what do you think *ordeal* means?
   - Ⓐ painful experience
   - Ⓑ trial to determine guilt or innocence
   - Ⓒ happy experience

5. In which sentence does the context fit the mood that is associated with *devastation?*
   - Ⓐ The people rejoiced at the devastation.
   - Ⓑ They happily accepted the devastation.
   - Ⓒ People cried and screamed when they saw the terrible devastation.

6. If a mall manager *banished* a group of troublemakers from the mall, what did he do?
   - Ⓐ Told them to go away and never come back
   - Ⓑ Invited them to stay longer
   - Ⓒ Reported them to the security officer

7. According to the passage, what is the definition of *salvation?*
   - Ⓐ rescue
   - Ⓑ danger
   - Ⓒ trust

8. What is a synonym for *crisis?*
   - Ⓐ habit
   - Ⓑ event
   - Ⓒ emergency

② Review Word Meanings

Read the passage below. Then answer the questions about the boldfaced vocabulary words.

Cholera

Cholera was one of many diseases that made the lives of American settlers and Native Americans difficult. Its symptoms included diarrhea and vomiting, and therefore it **deprived** victims of body fluids. Its final outcome was **unpredictable**—it was hard to tell whether someone with cholera would survive. Because cholera is mainly spread as a result of a dirty water supply, it still occurs in areas where people are **destitute** and cannot afford to live in an area with clean water.

In the spring of 1849, settlers were moving west, with high hopes of finding gold in California. What many of them found was cholera, and their **optimism** faded when many settlers died along the way. They were utterly **dismayed** as the disease raged up and down the wagon trains, and some people were **reluctant** to complete their journey. **Morale** was at an all-time low when families had to bury loved ones along the trail. Those who were alive and had the infection were **stranded** by the side of the trail because others were afraid of getting the disease. Still the settlers moved on, showing strength and **perseverance.**

Now read the following questions. Then completely fill in the bubble of the correct answer.

1. Which example sentence would be correct as a dictionary entry for *dismayed?*
   - Ⓐ The baseball team was dismayed when they won the championship.
   - Ⓑ The family was dismayed when their house was broken into.
   - Ⓒ The patient was dismayed when the doctor said that she was fine.

2. Which word is an antonym for *destitute?*
   - Ⓐ rich
   - Ⓑ happy
   - Ⓒ poor

3. What connotation does the word *reluctant* have?
   - Ⓐ positive
   - Ⓑ neutral
   - Ⓒ negative

4. Who was "*stranded* by the side of the trail?"
   - Ⓐ those who were tired
   - Ⓑ those who were alive and had the infection
   - Ⓒ those who were traveling alone

5. Cholera *deprived* victims of _____.
   - Ⓐ food
   - Ⓑ body fluids
   - Ⓒ water

6. Which of the following groups of words might you find in a thesaurus entry for *perseverance?*
   - Ⓐ strength, power, energy
   - Ⓑ determination, persistence, steadfastness
   - Ⓒ stubbornness, pig-headedness, inflexibility

7. What is an antonym for *optimism?*
   - Ⓐ hope
   - Ⓑ blind
   - Ⓒ hopelessness

8. According to the passage, what does *unpredictable* mean?
   - Ⓐ final outcome
   - Ⓑ hard to tell
   - Ⓒ with high hopes

3 Review Word Meanings

Read the passage below. Then answer the questions about the boldfaced vocabulary words.

Smallpox

The greatest **menace** that the Spanish explorers brought with them to the New World was the deadliest disease that the native population of the Americas would ever see—smallpox. When the Spanish, led by Hernán Cortés, tried to take over the Aztec empire, the **indignant** Aztecs drove them away and became **cynical** of foreign visitors. **Humiliated,** Cortés returned some ten years later, after the disease had hit the Aztecs with astounding **severity.** He and his men easily captured the city.

When Cortés originally attacked the Aztec capital, he had only 300 men to fight against 300,000 Aztecs. But smallpox had killed half the Aztec population, and the remaining were so sick and frightened that they could hardly put up a fight. By some accounts, some Spanish soldiers showed **apathy** toward the plight of the Aztecs, caring only about getting the riches. Some were even **jovial** because they did not have to fight in battle. The Aztec empire, and others like it, was conquered not by a **triumphant** army, but by a disease.

Now read the following questions. Then completely fill in the bubble of the correct answer.

1. Why did the Aztecs become *cynical?*
   - Ⓐ because they did not have rain
   - Ⓑ because Cortes brought them gifts
   - Ⓒ because Cortes tried to take over their empire

2. What root does the word *apathy* have, and what does it mean?
   - Ⓐ *pat,* which means "to pet"
   - Ⓑ *pathos,* which means "suffering" or "feeling"
   - Ⓒ *path,* which means "road"

3. According to the passage, what was the "greatest menace?"
   - Ⓐ smallpox
   - Ⓑ chicken pox
   - Ⓒ measles

4. What is another way of saying that some soldiers were *jovial?*
   - Ⓐ Some soldiers were happy.
   - Ⓑ Some soldiers were tired.
   - Ⓒ Some soldiers were scared.

5. In which sentence is the adjective form of the word *severity* used correctly?
   - Ⓐ The disease severely reduced the Native American populations.
   - Ⓑ Smallpox was the most severe illness that most Native American populations had ever known.
   - Ⓒ Smallpox and other severous diseases affected their way of life.

6. Study each word and its definition below. Which word do you think comes from the same Latin word as *humiliation?*
   - Ⓐ *humorous:* funny
   - Ⓑ *humanize:* to make human
   - Ⓒ *humble:* not proud

7. In the passage, what kind of army did *not* conquer the Aztecs?
   - Ⓐ triumphant
   - Ⓑ indignant
   - Ⓒ humiliated

8. What is a synonym for *vengeance?*
   - Ⓐ acceptance
   - Ⓑ happiness
   - Ⓒ revenge

④ Review Word Meanings

Read the passage below. Then answer the questions about the boldfaced vocabulary words.

Finding a Cure

Throughout history, **conscientious** doctors have tried to find cures for deadly diseases. For example, with each new outbreak of cholera in London, Dr. John Snow wanted to find, at the very least, a way to keep the disease from spreading. When cholera hit a section of the city in 1854, Dr. Snow **endeavored** to find the source. He gave the issue much **contemplation** and knew that he needed an **ingenious** idea.

Dr. Snow noticed that the disease seemed to show itself in the poorer sections of the city that were **cramped.** His **intuition** told him to track each new case using a map. Sure enough, all the new victims were located near one public water pump. He succeeded in getting the pump removed, even though there was much **dissatisfaction** among the people who needed water. The public was very **skeptical,** unconvinced that the disease was transmitted through the water supply. But soon the outbreak stopped. Today, Dr. Snow's tracking of a cholera outbreak to its source is seen as a great **accomplishment.** It also prompted governments to adopt more **rigorous** control of water supplies and other things that affected public health.

Now read the following questions. Then completely fill in the bubble of the correct answer.

1. In the passage, what is the meaning of *rigorous?*
   Ⓐ strict
   Ⓑ tough
   Ⓒ harsh

2. What is an antonym for *skeptical?*
   Ⓐ doubtful
   Ⓑ sure
   Ⓒ uncertain

3. According to the passage, what does the word *contemplation* mean?
   Ⓐ deep thought
   Ⓑ exercise
   Ⓒ organization

4. Which of the following would a *conscientious* doctor do?
   Ⓐ give the patient the wrong medication
   Ⓑ check in on a patient after surgery to explain how it went
   Ⓒ overcharge the insurance company

5. The closest synonym to *accomplishment* is
   Ⓐ achievement
   Ⓑ event
   Ⓒ ability

6. According to the passage, what is the definition of *intuition?*
   Ⓐ a part of the brain that controls higher thought processes
   Ⓑ a reflex
   Ⓒ an understanding of something without thinking about it

7. In the passage, what kind of idea did Dr. Snow have?
   Ⓐ humorous
   Ⓑ ingenious
   Ⓒ strange

8. In which year did Dr. Snow *endeavor* to find the source of cholera?
   Ⓐ 1554
   Ⓑ 1845
   Ⓒ 1854

Ancient Civilizations

1 Word Meanings

Restatement

 Read each sentence below. Circle the definition, or restatement, of each boldfaced vocabulary word.

1. artifact
(är′ tə fakt′) *n.*
product of human skill

2. anthropology
(an′ thrə pol′ ə jē) *n.*
science of human cultures

3. archaeology
(är′ kē ol′ ə jē) *n.*
scientific study of remains of past human life

4. evolve
(i volv′) *v.*
to develop gradually

5. excavation
(eks′ kə vā′ shən) *n.*
site of digging

6. chronological
(kron′ ə loj′ i kəl) *adj.*
in time order

7. hieroglyphics
(hī′ ər ə glif′ iks) *n.*
picture symbols

8. petrify
(pet′ rə fī′) *v.*
to turn to stone

9. monument
(mon′ yə mənt) *n.*
memorial structure

10. rituals
(rich′ o͞o əlz) *n.*
customs; ceremonies

1. In the United States, Lewis Henry Morgan was a founder of **anthropology.** This science of human cultures emerged as a separate field of study in the mid 1800s.

2. Biologists study how plants and animals **evolve,** or gradually develop, over time.

3. During the field trip to the museum, the students got a chance to see Egyptian **artifacts**—products of human skill.

4. Some people believe that **archaeology,** the scientific study of past human remains, is a branch of anthropology.

5. Archaeologists sometimes use past remains to figure out the order in which events occurred. By knowing this **chronological** order, they can better understand the cultures that they are studying.

6. The **excavation** of King Tut's tomb was dangerous. Many accidents occurred at the digging site.

7. A **monument** in northwestern New Mexico is a site of special importance because it preserves the ruins of a great Native American pueblo.

8. Anthropologists study the **rituals,** or social customs, of a group of people.

9. Scientists were amazed to see how the lava from Vesuvius was able to **petrify,** or turn to stone, the people and animals who lived in Pompeii.

10. Anthropologists have been fascinated by Egyptian **hieroglyphics** because these word symbols reveal valuable information about ancient Egypt.

② Reference Skills

Quotation Dictionary

 Read the following entry from a dictionary of quotations. Then read and answer each question below. Use a dictionary, if necessary.

> "I read a lot of archaeology and early history in a general way, not thinking particularly of this book, and this provided me with the background. It showed me how, possibly, the people lived back then." —Naomi Mitchison (1897–1999), Scottish novelist, "Interview with Naomi Mitchison," by Raymond H. Thompson, April 15, 1989.

1. Which vocabulary word is used in the quotation?

   _____ What does it mean in this context?

   _____

2. Who is the author of this quotation?

   _____

3. Where did this quotation appear?

   _____

4. Some quotation dictionaries are arranged by subject. Would this quotation appear under history?

   _____

   Scotland? _____

5. When was the author born? _____

6. When did the author say this quotation?

   _____

7. What was the author's profession?

   _____

8. Who conducted the interview?

   _____

Vocabulary List

1. artifact

2. anthropology

3. archaeology

4. evolve

5. excavation

6. chronological

7. hieroglyphics

8. petrify

9. monument

10. rituals

③ Build New Vocabulary

Word Parts

 Following are some of the word parts and their meanings that are used in this lesson's vocabulary words. Use these word parts to make new words and write them in the blanks. Use a dictionary, if necessary.

evolve: *volvere* (to roll)

1. *re-* (backward, again) + *volvere* = _____: *to move in a circle*

2. *in-* (into, toward) + *volvere* = _____: *to include as a necessary part, condition, or result*

3. *de-* (from, away) + *volvere* = _____: *to transfer work or responsibility to another*

chronological: *chrono-* (time)

4. *chrono-* + *meter* (measure) = _____: *timepiece*

5. *syn-* (together) + *chrono-* + *-ize* (to cause to be) =

   _____: *to happen at the same time*

6. *chrono-* + *logy* (to write) = _____: *a record of events in time order*

7. *ana-* (against) + *chrono* + *-ism* (state or condition) =

   _____: *out of place in the current time*

anthropology: *anthrop-* (human being); *-logy* (study of; science)

8. *misein* (to hate) + *anthrop* = _____: *someone who hates mankind*

9. *bio-* (life) + *-logy* = _____: *the science of life*

10. *geo-* (earth) + *-logy* = _____: *the study of the earth*

 **4** **Word Play**

Ideograms

 For each ideogram below, write the vocabulary word that best matches the symbol that is shown. For the last two items, the vocabulary word is given. Draw a symbol that represents each word.

1. _____

5. _____

2. _____

6. _____

3. _____

7. evolve

4. _____

8. artifact

Vocabulary List

1. **rejuvenate**
   (ri jōō′ və nāt′) *v.*
   to make young

2. **descent**
   (di sent′) *n.*
   ancestry

3. **adolescent**
   (ad′ ə les′ ənt) *n.*
   teenager; youth

4. **immortal**
   (i mor′ təl) *adj.*
   living forever

5. **vital**
   (vi′ təl) *adj.*
   relating to life;
   important

6. **inanimate**
   (in an′ ə mit) *adj.*
   without life; unmoving

7. **organism**
   (or′ gə niz′ əm) *n.*
   living thing

8. **existence**
   (eg zis′ təns) *n.*
   the condition of
   being real; life

9. **extinct**
   (ek stingkt′) *adj.*
   no longer surviving

10. **perish**
    (per′ ish) *v.*
    to die

"Life Cycle" Vocabulary

1 **Word Meanings**

Association

 Write the vocabulary word that fits best in each sentence.
Each word is used once.

1. Dinosaurs are _____, but their remains have been discovered around the world.

2. The Fountain of Youth is said to _____ anyone who drinks water from it.

3. If a forest fire is not controlled, everything in its path will

   _____.

4. Even though Elvis Presley is not alive today, he will always be

   _____ through his music.

5. A rock is an _____ object because it is incapable of moving on its own.

6. It is _____ to provide pets with food and water every day.

7. The _____ of the British royalty can be traced back to Germany and France.

8. Learning how to drive is part of being an

   _____.

9. There have been many tales about the _____ of aliens from other planets.

10. A whale is an _____ that lives in the ocean.

② Reference Skills

Multiple Meanings

Read the dictionary entries for *descent* and *vital* below. Then read each sentence and fill in each blank with the correct word. In the box write the number of the definition for the word that you used.

---

descent *n.* **1.** movement from a higher place to a lower one: *the descent of the elevator.* **2.** downward slope or inclination: *a hill with a steep descent.* **3.** ancestry or birth: *That family is of Russian descent.* **4.** A sudden attack

vital *adj.* **1.** relating to or characteristic of life: *vital systems.* **2.** necessary for maintaining life: *vital organs, vital fluids.* **3.** full of life; energetic: *vital character.* **4.** essential; of the utmost importance: *Practice is vital to the success of our team.* **5.** deadly; destructive to life: *vital wound.*

---

1. Shaunté found out that she was of African and Puerto Rican

   _____. ☐

2. Many people live _____, satisfying lives. ☐

3. The Vikings made their _____ on the village at

   dawn. ☐

4. Anne Frank's father thought that it was _____

   to go into hiding or somehow get out of the country. ☐

5. The grizzly bear made a _____ tear in the

   hunter's leg. ☐

6. Elijah was scared to ride his bike down the long

   _____. ☐

Vocabulary List

1. rejuvenate

2. descent

3. adolescent

4. immortal

5. vital

6. inanimate

7. organism

8. existence

9. extinct

10. perish

 3 Build New Vocabulary

Word Parts

Study the meaning of each root and suffix below. Use this information to match each word in the first column with its meaning in the second column. Look up each word in the dictionary to check your answers.

Roots	Suffixes
vita: life	**-ity:** quality or state
vivere: to live	**-ous:** full of; abounding
mort-, mors-: death	**-ian:** one who is of, related to, or skilled in
	-fy: to make; form into
	-ary: thing connected to, especially a place

1. vitality   **A.** to animate; make lively

2. vivify   **B.** funeral home

3. vivacious   **C.** undertaker

4. mortuary   **D.** lively

5. mortify   **E.** animation; liveliness

6. mortician   **F.** destroy

• •

 Circle the word in parentheses that correctly completes the sentences below.

7. After a drought, farmers hope that a rainstorm will *(mortify/vivify)* their crops.

8. A *(mortuary/mortician)* is a person who assists families when they have to make funeral arrangements.

Word Play

Analogies

Study the relationships between the words in each analogy below. Determine the relationship between the words in the complete pair and write it in the blank. Then write the vocabulary word that completes the incomplete pair so that the relationship is the same as the relationship in the complete pair.

1. _____ is to *breakdown* as *young* is to *old*.

_____

2. _____ is to *short-lived* as *powerful* is to *weak*.

_____

3. _____ is to *life* as *mortal* is to *death*.

_____

4. _____ is to *rock* as *living* is to *animal*.

_____

5. *Died out* is to _____ as *alive* is to *living*.

_____

6. *Live* is to _____ as *thrive* is to *die*.

_____

7. *Teenager* is to _____ as *baby* is to *infant*.

_____

8. _____ is to *nothingness* as *light* is to *dark*.

_____

1. initiate
(i nish´ ē āt´) *v.*
to begin or introduce

2. duration
(dŏŏ rā´ shən) *n.*
length of time

3. imminent
(im´ ə nənt) *adj.*
about to happen

4. tentative
(ten´ tə tiv) *adj.*
not decided; uncertain

5. resume
(ri zōōm´) *v.*
to go on with

6. simultaneous
(sī´ məl tā´ nē əs) *adj.*
at the same time

7. punctual
(pungk´ chōō əl) *adj.*
on time

8. recur
(ri kûr´) *v.*
to happen again

9. terminate
(tûr´ mə nāt´) *v.*
to bring to an end

10. span
(span) *n.*
space of time

"Time" Vocabulary

 1 Word Meanings

Word Choice

 Circle the vocabulary word in parentheses that correctly completes each sentence.

1. The *(span/duration)* of the American Civil War was 1861–1865.

2. The student was *(imminent/punctual)* for class.

3. Rashida had to *(recur/initiate)* the discussion between her mother and sister.

4. The umpire had to *(resume/terminate)* the game after the rain stopped.

5. The judge told the lawyer to *(recur/terminate)* her examination of the witness.

6. The *(duration/span)* of the movie is two hours and ten minutes.

7. Abigail has *(punctual/tentative)* plans for Friday night.

8. The sky divers made a *(tentative/simultaneous)* jump.

9. Lunch will *(recur/terminate)* at the same time tomorrow.

10. Fred was afraid of the *(simultaneous/imminent)* danger in the woods.

● ●

Think About It

Did you reread each sentence after you circled the answer? Make sure the word fits with the context of the sentence.

② Reference Skills

Multiple Meanings

Following are entries from a thesaurus for three of the vocabulary words. Cross-check in a dictionary the meaning of each synonym that is listed in the entries. Then replace the boldfaced vocabulary word in each sentence below with the synonym that best completes the sentence. Change the form of the words, as necessary.

> **initiate** *v.:* launch, inform, teach, enlighten
> **terminate** *v.:* discontinue, complete, conclude
> **tentative** *adj.:* conditional, temporary, uncertain

1. Eleanor Roosevelt **initiated** her own political career by joining the League of Women voters around 1918. _____

2. Eleanor wanted to **initiate** others about social issues around the world. _____

3. When her husband died, Mrs. Roosevelt did not **terminate** her involvement in politics. _____

4. Franklin and Eleanor were not **tentative** about marrying, for they were in love. _____

5. Franklin did not **terminate** his law degree despite passing the state law exams. _____

6. French-speaking and German-speaking tutors **initiated** young Franklin Roosevelt. _____

7. Franklin Delano Roosevelt's role as president was not **tentative;** he served four terms as leader of the United States.

   _____

8. Franklin Delano Roosevelt was not alive to see the **termination** of World War II. _____

1. *initiate*

2. *duration*

3. *imminent*

4. *tentative*

5. *resume*

6. *simultaneous*

7. *punctual*

8. *recur*

9. *terminate*

10. *span*

 3 **Build New Vocabulary**

Suffixes

 Combine each vocabulary word below with the suffix shown to form a new word. Write the new word in the blank.

1. initiate + -ion = _____: *the act of beginning; proceedings during which someone is made a member of a group*

2. initiate + -ive = _____: *lead; first step*

3. terminate + -ion = _____: *end; firing from a job*

4. punctual + -ity = _____: *promptness; the act of arriving on time*

5. simultaneous + -ly = _____: *happening at the same time*

• •

 Correctly complete each sentence below by writing one of the new words that you formed above.

6. _____ is an important characteristic for a bus driver.

7. The company was running out of money, so the

_____ of its employees would soon follow.

8. When asked whether they wanted ice cream, the girls

_____ answered, "Yes!"

9. The boy looked forward to his _____ into the club.

10. By signing up for classes, Emilia took the

_____ to get a college degree.

4 Word Play

Idioms

 Choose the idiom from the box below that best fits each sentence and write the idiom in the blank. Look up keywords in the dictionary or an idiom dictionary if you are unsure of the meanings of the idioms.

Idioms	
all over but the shouting	Let's roll
game on	until the cows come home
shake a leg	just around the corner
neck and neck	test the waters

1. Someone who is *punctual* might tell you to

   _____.

2. If you want to *initiate* an action, you might tell a group of people,

   "_____."

3. If you are ready to *resume* your street hockey game, you might say,

   "_____."

4. If you are willing to stay somewhere for a long *duration*, you might tell

   someone that you will stay _____.

5. If you and your friend reach the finish line *simultaneously*,
   you might say that the two of you were

   _____.

6. If your dad's promotion is *imminent*, he might tell your family that

   it is _____.

7. Someone who is *tentative* might

   _____ before taking action.

8. If a war is near its *termination*, a general might say that it's

   _____.

1. **residue**
   (rez´ i dōō´) *n.*
   remaining substance

2. **corrosion**
   (kə rō´ zhən) *n.*
   wearing away

3. **evaporate**
   (i vap´ ə rāt´) *v.*
   to change into vapor

4. **adhesive**
   (ad hē´ siv) *n.*
   sticky substance

5. **insoluble**
   (in sol´ yə bəl) *adj.*
   unable to be dissolved

6. **dilute**
   (di lōōt´) *v.*
   to thin or weaken

7. **condensed**
   (kən denst´) *adj.*
   thickened

8. **procedure**
   (prə sē´ jər) *n.*
   way of doing

9. **reactor**
   (rē ak´ tər) *n.*
   device used to produce
   atomic energy

10. **metamorphosis**
    (met´ ə mor´ fə sis) *n.*
    change of form

Science Vocabulary

1 Word Meanings

Questions

 Answer each question below using the vocabulary words.

1. What type of substance is glue?

   a(n) _____

2. What happens to a caterpillar when it changes into a butterfly?

   _____

3. What is it called when salt water makes holes in a boat?

   _____

4. What do you do when you add water to juice to make it less sweet?

   _____

5. What type of machine creates powerful energy?

   a(n) _____

6. What kind of milk has been thickened?

   _____

7. What is sometimes left on a surface after you clean it?

   _____

8. How do you change water into steam?

   _____

9. Why is a rock unable to dissolve in water?

   _____

10. What do you have to follow when you do a science experiment?

    a(n) _____

② Reference Skills

Multiple Meanings

 Read the dictionary entries for the words below. Then complete each sentence with the correct form of one of the words. Write the number of the definition that you used in the box.

---

adhesive *adj.* **1.** tending to stick to or hold fast; clinging: *Paste and glue have adhesive properties.* **2.** having a sticky surface that will hold fast to something; gummed: *an adhesive label. n.* **1.** a sticky substance: *Paste is an adhesive.*

condense *v.* **1.** to thicken or reduce the volume of: *condense gravy by boiling it.* **2.** to shorten and make more succinct: *condense a story.* **3.** to change gas to a liquid or solid

insoluble *adj.* **1.** incapable of being dissolved: *an insoluble substance.* **2.** incapable of being solved: *an insoluble crime.*

---

1. Sherlock Holmes rarely thought that a murder mystery was

   _____. ☐

2. Water droplets form when water vapor

   _____. ☐

3. The reporter had to put an _____ name tag on

   her shirt. ☐

4. A piece of gum is _____ in a glass of

   water. ☐

5. *Reader's Digest* _____ stories for people who

   don't have time to read the longer versions. ☐

6. If you have bubble gum on your shoes, your shoes have

   _____ qualities. ☐

Vocabulary List

1. residue
2. corrosion
3. evaporate
4. adhesive
5. insoluble
6. dilute
7. condensed
8. procedure
9. reactor
10. metamorphosis

3 Build New Vocabulary

Noun Forms

 Add the suffix *-ion* to each vocabulary word below to form a noun that matches the definition that is provided.

1. adhesive + *-ion* _____: *the act of sticking*

2. dilute + *-ion* _____: *the act of weakening or thinning by adding a liquid*

3. condense + *-ion* _____: *the changing of a gas to a liquid*

4. evaporate + *-ion* _____: *the changing of a liquid to a gas*

• •

 Complete each sentence below by writing one of the new words you formed above.

5. Postage stamps have _____.

6. The _____ of water occurs quickly on hot, dry days.

7. Dew is _____ that forms in small drops during the night on grass and other cool surfaces.

8. The _____ of sports drinks with water helps athletes replenish body fluids quickly.

• •

 Answer the following questions.

9. Which vocabulary word already has the *-ion* ending?

_____

10. What is its verb form?

_____

Word Play

Word Puzzle

 Write the vocabulary word that fits each clue below.

1. It is kind of sticky.

☐☐☐☐☐☐☐☐

2. vanish into thin air

☐☐☐☐☐☐☐☐☐

3. What is left?

☐☐☐☐☐☐☐

4. a change in form

☐☐☐☐☐☐☐☐☐☐☐☐

5. what an old car has on it

☐☐☐☐☐☐☐☐☐

6. what a mystery sometimes is

☐☐☐☐☐☐☐☐☐

7. soup that needs water added

☐☐☐☐☐☐☐☐

Unscramble the circled letters from above to answer the question below.

8. What does an ant with heartburn drink?

☐☐☐☐☐☐☐

1. **expansive**
(ek span´ siv) *adj.*
extending widely

2. **taper**
(tā´ pər) *v.*
to make gradually
narrower

3. **inverted**
(in vûrt´ id) *adj.*
reversed in position

4. **magnitude**
(mag´ ni tōōd´) *n.*
size

5. **cylindrical**
(sə lin´ dri kəl) *adj.*
shaped like a cylinder;
long and round

6. **perpendicular**
(pûr´ pən dik´ yə lər)
adj.
at right angles

7. **congruent**
(kong´ grōō ənt) *adj.*
exactly the same in
size and shape

8. **elongate**
(i lông´ gāt) *v.*
to lengthen

9. **parallel**
(par´ ə lel´) *adj.*
always equal distance
apart; never touching

10. **spherical**
(sfer´ i kəl) *adj.*
shaped like a ball

Size and Shape

 Word Meanings

Categorization

Read each group of examples listed below and choose the vocabulary word that best describes each group. Write the vocabulary word in the blank. Look up any words and phrases if you are unsure of their meaning.

1. _____: baseball, globe, marble

2. _____: lines on a football field, lanes on a highway, stripes on the flag

3. _____: identical twins, stars on the American flag, compact discs

4. _____: someone standing on his or her head, a pyramid standing on its point; the fraction 3/4 compared to 4/3

5. _____: width, height, weight

6. _____: can of soup, drinking glass, paper-towel roll

7. _____: sidewalks that meet at a corner, longitude in relation to latitude, the lines in the letter *T*

8. _____: Pinocchio's nose, The Beanstalk, Alice in Wonderland after she eats a mushroom

9. _____: a pyramid, the Washington Monument, pant legs

10. _____: desert, rolling farmland, ocean

 Think About It

What are some other examples that belong in these categories?

② Reference Skills

Visualization

 Dictionaries sometimes use an illustration to add to the meaning of a definition. Draw an illustration for each of the vocabulary words below.

1. two **congruent** triangles

3. two **perpendicular** lines

2. two **parallel** lines

4. an **inverted** birthday cake

 Circle the correct illustration for each vocabulary word below

5. spherical

6. cylindrical

Vocabulary List

1. *expansive*
2. *taper*
3. *inverted*
4. *magnitude*
5. *cylindrical*
6. *perpendicular*
7. *congruent*
8. *elongate*
9. *parallel*
10. *spherical*

3 Build New Vocabulary

Context Clues

 The Latin word *versus* means "turning." Following are words based on the word *versus* along with prefixes and suffixes. For each numbered item below, write the correct word from the box in the blank.

inverted	diversion	introvert	versatile	reverse

1. *re-* (back) + *versus* = _____

2. *in-* (into) + *versus* = _____

3. *di-* (apart) + *versus* + *-ion* (act or process) =

   _____

4. *versus-* + *-ile* (capable of) = _____

5. *intro-* (to the inside) + *versus* = _____

• •

 Complete each sentence below by writing one of the new words you formed above.

6. Because of his many interests, hobbies, and skills, Theodore Roosevelt is considered to be one of our most

   _____ presidents.

7. He was energetic, sociable, and outgoing—anything but an

   _____ .

8. An enthusiastic hiker, hunter, reader, and more, Roosevelt had many

   _____ to keep him busy.

9. Some nationalists hoped that Roosevelt would

   _____ his opinion about annexing Cuba.

10. Never a fan of Woodrow Wilson's, Roosevelt never

   _____ his opinion of him.

Word Play

Tongue Twisters

 Read each tongue twister below. Fill in the blanks with the vocabulary word that best fits. Words may be used only once.

1. Tin-Lun wanted to _____ his tattered trousers.

2. Explorers examined an _____ area of Earth.

3. Edgar the elephant had to _____ his trunk to elevate the egg.

4. _____ seashells sat shining in the sand.

5. A couple of cousins copied _____ clouds on colored canvas.

6. Pamela placed pencils in a _____ pattern.

7. Inga inked illustrations of _____ igloos.

8. Pavers plowed _____ paths.

9. Manuel and Monica marveled at the _____ of the mangoes and watermelons.

10. Stella saw Simon and Sonja standing near a

   _____ silo.

• •

 Think About It

What tongue twisters do you know? Does this one sound familiar? *I thought a thought. But the thought I thought wasn't the thought I thought.*

Vocabulary Review

1 **Review Word Meanings**

Read the passage below. Then answer the questions about the boldfaced vocabulary words.

Uncovering the Past

To people in the field of **archaeology,** digging through the bones and buried treasure of past civilizations is all in a day's work. In addition, most archaeologists are also interested in **anthropology,** because knowing how humans developed helps them understand what they find. Sometimes an important site is found by accident—a construction worker might uncover a human skeleton, for example—and archaeologists begin their **excavation.** They carefully dig, often with many different people working **simultaneously** in different areas.

When first beginning an excavation, archaeologists often divide the area into **congruent** squares, or a grid. They measure rows of equal width, perhaps first going east and west, so they are **parallel,** like the yards of a football field. Then, going north to south, they mark rows that are **perpendicular** to the first set of rows, creating squares in which they can dig. Archaeologists search for **monuments** that might reveal important **rituals,** bones, or anything that might give a clue about the people who once lived at the site.

Now read the following questions. Then completely fill in the bubble of the correct answer.

1. Which two vocabulary words from the passage fall under the category of *Sciences?*
   - Ⓐ monuments, archaeology
   - Ⓑ archaeology, rituals
   - Ⓒ archaeology, anthropology

2. According to the passage, what is the definition of *congruent?*
   - Ⓐ exactly alike in size and shape
   - Ⓑ large in size
   - Ⓒ shaped like a triangle

3. Finish the following analogy with a vocabulary word from the passage: *Astronomy* is to *planets and stars* as _____ is to *human beings.*
   - Ⓐ archaeology
   - Ⓑ anthropology
   - Ⓒ excavation

4. According to the passage, what is the definition of *simultaneous?*
   - Ⓐ at different times
   - Ⓑ confident
   - Ⓒ at the same time

5. In which sentence below is *excavate* correctly defined?
   - Ⓐ Archaeologists excavate, or clean, buried skeletons.
   - Ⓑ Archaeologists excavate, or unearth, buried skeletons.
   - Ⓒ Archaeologists excavate, or measure, buried skeletons.

6. Which are examples of *monuments?*
   - Ⓐ gravestones, statues, and towers
   - Ⓑ tubas, violins, drums
   - Ⓒ bones, artifacts, ruins

7. A monument might reveal important _____.
   - Ⓐ archaeologists
   - Ⓑ squares
   - Ⓒ rituals

8. According to the passage, which of the following are *parallel?*
   - Ⓐ yards on a football field
   - Ⓑ monuments
   - Ⓒ digs

Score _____ (Top Score 8)

② Review Word Meanings

Read the passage below. Then answer the questions about the boldfaced vocabulary words.

City Buried by a Volcano

One city that fascinates archaeologists is Herculaneum, a city of ancient Italy. Most of its inhabitants **perished** when the top of a volcano, Vesuvius, which lay three miles away, exploded and covered the city with ashes and mud. **Vital** information about the eruption was recorded by a 17-year-old student named Pliny the Younger.

From across the **expanse** of the Bay of Naples in Misenum, Pliny the Younger described the horrific sight. He wrote of earth shocks so strong that Earth seemed to be **inverted** and of watching **spherical** clouds of ash rise up. For the **duration** of the earthquake, people in Misenum spoke of their own **imminent** deaths. There was no way to **dilute** the truth—sheets of fire and ash were flashing out of Vesuvius, which was only 20 miles across the bay. A popular resort city for rich Romans, Herculaneum was wiped out of **existence** with one violent eruption. By the time the explosion calmed down, those inhabitants that had not fled were killed by blasts of hot gases and buried under ash.

Now read the following questions. Then completely fill in the bubble of the correct answer.

1. In which sentence below is *dilute* used the same way that it is used in the passage?
   Ⓐ Parents sometimes dilute juice with water before giving it to babies.
   Ⓑ The house cleaner uses water to dilute the bleach.
   Ⓒ The father diluted the impact of his scolding by smiling halfway through.

2. According to the passage, what is the dictionary definition of *existence?*
   Ⓐ the state or fact of being
   Ⓑ the way out
   Ⓒ a departure

3. When did most of the inhabitants of Herculaneum *perish?*
   Ⓐ when Mount Rushmore exploded
   Ⓑ when Mount St. Helens exploded
   Ⓒ when Vesuvius exploded

4. *Momentary* could be used as a synonym for which of the following words from the passage?
   Ⓐ duration
   Ⓑ inverted
   Ⓒ imminent

5. In which sentence below is *vital* used the same way it is in the passage?
   Ⓐ The vital organs include your heart, brain, and lungs.
   Ⓑ The soldier suffered a vital wound and knew that he would die.
   Ⓒ Nutritious food is vital to the development of children.

6. Which word below could be used as a synonym for *invert?*
   Ⓐ overturn
   Ⓑ change
   Ⓒ discuss

7. Which sentence below would be correct in a dictionary entry for *spherical?*
   Ⓐ Earth is spherical in shape.
   Ⓑ A cube is spherical in shape.
   Ⓒ An egg is spherical in shape.

8. "From across the expanse of the Bay of Naples in Misenum, Pliny the Younger described the horrific sight." If this quote appeared in a quotation dictionary, which word or phrase below might help you locate it?
   Ⓐ earthquake
   Ⓑ Pliny the Younger
   Ⓒ description

③ Review Word Meanings

Read the passage below. Then answer the questions about the boldfaced vocabulary words.

The Bone Lady

Archaeologist Dr. Sara Bisel, called "the bone lady" because of her ability to "read" bones, wrote about her work at Herculaneum in *The Secrets of Vesuvius*. In June of 1982, the National Geographic Society contacted her, asking her to **initiate** work at Herculaneum as soon as possible. A worker had accidentally discovered some skeletons while digging a ditch at a site that was just past the edge of the ruins. Dr. Bisel was not **tentative** about her answer—she did not have to think about rejecting the offer.

Wanting to be **punctual,** she hopped on the next flight to Naples to study skeletons that had been around since ancient times. But she didn't arrive until nighttime—one needed daylight to work at the site—so she decided to read about Vesuvius and Herculaneum and **resume** her work in the morning. Dr. Bisel wondered what the skeletons and **inanimate** objects found with them would tell her. What seemingly **insoluble** mystery would she solve? Would the **descent** of the skeleton be revealed? Sara had no idea what the **magnitude** of her findings would be.

- -

Now read the following questions. Then completely fill in the bubble of the correct answer.

1. If *animate* means "having life," what does *inanimate* mean?
   Ⓐ life within
   Ⓑ spirit
   Ⓒ without life

2. In which sentence below is a form of *punctual* used correctly?
   Ⓐ To keep their place at the restaurant, punctuality was a must.
   Ⓑ She was known for her punctualness.
   Ⓒ Some doctors are not known for their punctualation.

3. What is the definition of *tentative* as it is used in the passage?
   Ⓐ experimental
   Ⓑ uncertain
   Ⓒ not final

4. What did Dr. Bisel *resume* in the morning?
   Ⓐ her work
   Ⓑ her journey
   Ⓒ her flight

5. In which sentence below is a form of *initiate* used correctly?
   Ⓐ Her initiation into the field of archaeology took place in college.
   Ⓑ Her initial into the field of archaeology was a good experience.
   Ⓒ Her initiasion into the field of archaeology began at a young age.

6. In the passage, what does *insoluble* mean?
   Ⓐ cannot be dissolved
   Ⓑ cannot be solved
   Ⓒ cannot be consoled

7. According to the passage, which sentence below uses *descent* correctly?
   Ⓐ There was a steep descent.
   Ⓑ The descent from the tree was long.
   Ⓒ I come from Polish descent.

8. Which word below is a synonym of *magnitude?*
   Ⓐ size
   Ⓑ length
   Ⓒ width

④ Review Word Meanings

Read the passage below. Then answer the questions about the boldfaced vocabulary words.

The Skeletons of Herculaneum

In all, Dr. Sara Bisel examined 139 skeletons of people whose lives had been **terminated** by the volcano's explosion. For each bone, she would carefully brush off dirt or other **residue.** Sometimes she came across a jumble of bones and it was hard to tell how many different people they made up. She could tell a lot by studying the position of the bones—what had **evolved** in the minutes before the volcano finally took the victims' lives. By testing the bones for different substances, she could also tell the person's habits—whether he or she had an illness or what kind of diet he or she ate. Because the Herculaeans had no sugar in their diets, their teeth showed little sign of **corrosion.**

In addition to bones, Sara Bisel came across countless other objects of all shapes and sizes—**cylindrical** drinking vessels, **tapered** swords lying next to ancient soldiers. Although the people of Herculaneum came before us **chronologically,** they still live on through their well-preserved bones. Indeed, even though their bodies are gone, their story is **immortal** like the Roman gods they believed in.

Now read the following questions. Then completely fill in the bubble of the correct answer.

1. Which item falls under the category *Cylindrical?*
   - Ⓐ a drinking glass
   - Ⓑ a ball
   - Ⓒ a house

2. In which sentence below is *immortal* defined?
   - Ⓐ The ancient Romans believed that their gods were immortal.
   - Ⓑ Would you really want never to die—to be immortal?
   - Ⓒ The children acted as though they were immortal.

3. What type of swords did Dr. Bisel find?
   - Ⓐ cylindrical
   - Ⓑ terminated
   - Ⓒ tapered

4. In which sentence below is the noun form of *evolve* used correctly?
   - Ⓐ Archaeologists can tell us about the evolution of ancient cultures.
   - Ⓑ The teacher witnessed the teenager's evolution from a poor student to an excellent one.
   - Ⓒ The evolutionary of ancient cultures is fascinating.

5. Which sentence below would be correct in a dictionary entry for *residue?*
   - Ⓐ After the fire, there was a residue of ash everywhere.
   - Ⓑ She residued in a large city.
   - Ⓒ The residue demanded to see the mayor.

6. Which word could replace *terminated* in the passage?
   - Ⓐ started
   - Ⓑ extended
   - Ⓒ ended

7. According to the passage, who chronologically came first?
   - Ⓐ us
   - Ⓑ the people of Herculaneum
   - Ⓒ Dr. Sara Bissel

8. Which word below is a synonym for *corrosion?*
   - Ⓐ decay
   - Ⓑ life
   - Ⓒ brightness

1. **justification**
(jus´ tə fi kā´ shən) *n.*
a satisfactory reason

2. **reckon**
(rek´ ən) *v.*
to consider; to think

3. **denounce**
(di nouns´) *v.*
to attack publicly
with words

4. **retort**
(ri tort´) *v.*
to reply quickly
or sharply

5. **coax**
(kōks) *v.*
to persuade gently
or with flattery

6. **contradict**
(kon´ trə dikt´) *v.*
to say the opposite

7. **assertive**
(ə sûr´ tiv) *adj.*
aggresive or forward
in manner

8. **audacity**
(ô das´ i tē) *n.*
boldness or daring

9. **conform**
(kən form´) *v.*
to behave or think
like others

10. **rejection**
(ri jek´ shən) *n.*
refusal to accept
or believe

Taking a Stand

1 Word Meanings

Examples

For each sentence below, write the vocabulary word that best fits in the blank.

1. People who _____ might say, "We're doing it because everyone else is doing it."

2. Two people who _____ each other might have the following conversation: "Did not!" "Did too!"

3. Someone might _____ another person by saying, "I'm not afraid to tell all of you that he is a thief and a liar!"

4. Someone might _____ while saying, "Which box of cereal is the better value?"

5. Someone who is trying to _____ might say, "You're such a nice babysitter . . . Can I stay up one more hour?"

6. Someone who has _____ for not doing something might say, "Sorry I let you down, but I couldn't play because I had the chicken pox."

7. Someone who is _____ might say, "Would you please stop talking? I'm trying to watch this movie."

8. A boss might give an employee the following

   _____: "I cannot accept your explanation."

9. Someone who has _____ might say, "I know we just met, but could you lend me ten dollars?"

10. In response to the question "Where have you been all day?" a person

    might _____, "None of your business!"

2 Reference Skills

Proofreading

Proofread the sentences below for errors in spelling. Use a dictionary to find the correct spelling. Use proofreading marks to correct the errors.

Proofreading Marks

¶ – Indent.	^ – Add something.	ℰ – Take out something.
ᵔ – Transpose.	≡ – Make a capital letter.	/ – Make a small letter.
SP – Check spelling.	◯ – Close up a space.	⊙ – Add a period.

1. During the Vietnam War, some people who were for the war and some people who were against the war were very assirtive.

2. Called Doves, the people who were against the war deenownsed it.

3. They refused to kunform to the idea that the United States belonged in the war.

4. Some thought it kontradikted the ideals of the American people.

5. Some Hawks, or people for the war, reejekted the protests of the Doves.

6. They reetorted that everyone should support their boys fighting overseas.

7. Some believed that America was justafyed in being there.

8. Many soldiers coming back from the war reckined that they were just glad to be alive.

9. Some demonstrators tried to coaxe people into burning their draft cards.

10. The awdacity of some demonstrators got them in trouble with the law.

Vocabulary List

1. justification
2. reckon
3. denounce
4. retort
5. coax
6. contradict
7. assertive
8. audacity
9. conform
10. rejection

③ Build New Vocabulary

Affixes

For each root below make two new words using the affixes in the box. Some new words may be forms of the vocabulary words, and some may not. You will use some of the affixes more than once. Write each new word in the blank next to its definition. Use the dictionary to check your words.

Affixes

contra-:	against	*inter-:*	between
con-:	with; together	*re-:*	back; again
pre-:	before	*-ify:*	make; form into
de-:	opposite; from; down	*un-:*	not

Roots

1. *just:* right

   _____ to make right

   _____ not right

2. *ject:* throw

   _____ to throw back

   _____ to throw between

3. *dict:* to say

   _____ to say the opposite

   _____ to say what will happen before it happens

4. *form:* shape

   _____ to shape together

   _____ to disfigure

5. *nounce:* report

   _____ to report against

   _____ to formally give up

 **Word Play**

Word Charades

 Write the vocabulary word that answers each word charade.

1. This is when you say something and then five seconds later you say

   the opposite of what you just said. _____

2. You decide to fit in and do what everyone else is doing. This
   word also means that you agree to follow a rule.

   _____

3. This means flattering someone to try to get him or her to do
   something. You do this if you "twist someone's arm."

   _____

4. You quickly and bitingly respond to someone. This is a clever way to get
   back at someone who has said something rude to you.

   _____

5. An athlete who does not make the team after practicing for months
   or a person who is not allowed into a secret club might feel this.

   _____

6. You have this if you still ask for allowance money even though you
   did not clean your room or take out the garbage.

   _____

7. This word means "giving a good reason for doing something you

   might have been warned not to do." _____

8. To do this means to suppose something to be true.

   _____

9. Some people might call you pushy, but you are really just standing up

   for yourself if you are this way. _____

10. You do this if you are strongly against something and you make a

    public statement about it. _____

1. **appeal**
(ə pēl´) v.
to take to a higher court

2. **undergo**
(un´ dər gō´) v.
to experience;
to endure

3. **liberation**
(li´ bə rā´ shən) n.
freedom

4. **unrelenting**
(un´ ri len´ ting) adj.
harsh, unchanging

5. **oppressive**
(ə pres´ iv) adj.
cruel

6. **distort**
(di stort´) v.
to twist or bend out
of shape

7. **discrimination**
(di skrim´ ə nā´ shən) n.
unfair treatment

8. **rebel**
(ri bel´) v.
to resist or turn against

9. **proclaim**
(prə klām´) v.
to announce publicly

10. **displace**
(dis plās´) v.
to force to leave home

"Injustice" Vocabulary

① Word Meanings

Using Exact Words

 Draw a line through the boldfaced word or group of words below. Then write the vocabulary word that means the same as each boldfaced word or group of words.

1. Many northern politicians wanted to **request that a higher court review** the decision that legalized slavery.

2. On January 1, 1863, President Lincoln gave a speech to **say officially** that slaves in the South were free.

3. The South wanted to keep slavery, but the North did not. As a result,

   the South **turned against** against the North and tried to separate from the Union.

4. The slaves won their **freedom** because the North won the Civil War.

5. For years, slaves had to **experience** poor treatment because many Americans did not understand their culture.

6. Many people were **put out of their homes** after their homes were taken over by enemy troops.

7. In 1852, Harriet Beecher Stowe published *Uncle Tom's Cabin*, which illustrated the evils of slavery. In response, many Southerners said

   that the book did nothing but **twist or stretch** the truth about slavery.

8. Because of **unfair treatment** in the South, many newly freed slaves moved to the North, hoping to be treated more humanely.

9. Many slaves worked under **difficult and cruel** conditions. Consequently, some tried to escape to the North.

10. Because of the **harsh** summers in some southern states, some slaves collapsed from heat exhaustion.

2 Reference Skills

Multiple Meanings

 Read the dictionary entry below. Then write the correct definition of *rebel* in each blank based on the context of each sentence.

> **rebel** (*n., adj.,* reb′ əl; *v.,* ri bel′) *n.* **1.** a person who opposes or refuses to obey authority. **2. Rebel.** a person who fought for the Confederacy during the Civil War. *adj.* of or relating to people who refuse to obey authority: *rebel forces; rebel camp. v.* **re•belled, re•bel•ling 1.** to oppose or disobey authority. **2.** to feel or show strong dislike: *rebel against the inhumane treatment of animals.*

1. **Rebel** forces lost the Battle of Gettysburg in July 1863.

   _____

   _____

2. The movie ***Rebel** Without a Cause* was about a troubled teenager who fought with his parents and resisted school authorities.

   _____

   _____

3. During the Civil War, people who were called **Rebels** believed the South would win.

   _____

   _____

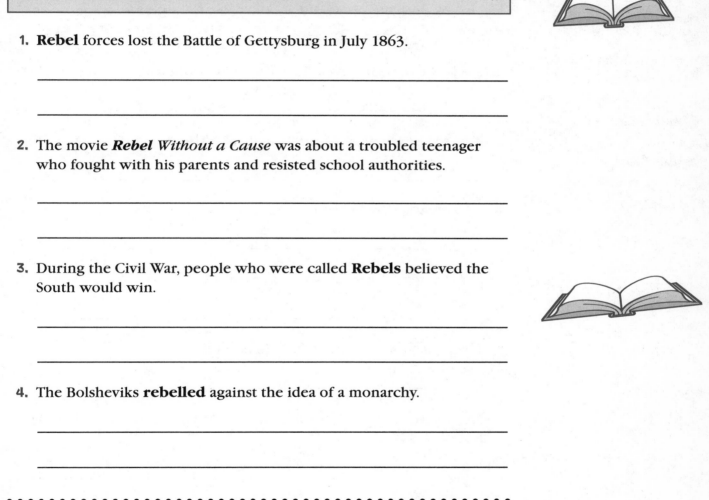

4. The Bolsheviks **rebelled** against the idea of a monarchy.

   _____

   _____

• •

 Think About It

How is the pronunciation of *rebel* different for each part of speech?

Vocabulary List

1. *appeal*
2. *undergo*
3. *liberation*
4. *unrelenting*
5. *oppressive*
6. *distort*
7. *discrimination*
8. *rebel*
9. *proclaim*
10. *displace*

3 Build New Vocabulary

Negative Prefixes

Study the negative prefixes and their meanings and uses in the box below. Add a negative prefix from the box to each boldfaced word and write its definition. Do not use the boldfaced word in your definition. Use a dictionary to check your answers.

---

un-: not; opposite of

dis-: opposite of; lack of; undo

non-: not; opposite of

in-, im-, ir-: without; not (Note: *in-* can also mean *in, into, on, with,* or *toward*) The prefix *in-* changes to *im-* before the letter *m* or *p*.

---

1. Ancient Greeks believed that gods were **mortal.**

   _____

2. Rocks are examples of objects that are **animate.**

   _____

3. A triangle and a circle are **congruent.**

   _____

4. Nancy Drew solves cases that seem **soluble.**

   _____

5. The path a tornado may take is **predictable.**

   _____

6. The colonists showed **content** with British tax laws by staging the Boston Tea Party.

   _____

7. The king of England thought that American colonists' opinions were **relevant.**

   _____

8. Abolitionists believed that slavery was **just.**

   _____

 **4** **Word Play**

Connotation

 Read each vocabulary word below. Decide if its connotation is more negative than positive, or more positive than negative. Circle the correct connotation for each word.

Connotation

		negative	positive
1.	appeal	negative	positive
2.	discrimination	negative	positive
3.	unrelenting	negative	positive
4.	oppressive	negative	positive
5.	distort	negative	positive
6.	liberation	negative	positive
7.	undergo	negative	positive
8.	rebel	negative	positive
9.	displace	negative	positive
10.	proclaim	negative	positive

Vocabulary List

1. **elusive**
   (i lōō′ siv) *adj.*
   hard to catch

2. **filthy**
   (fil′ thē) *adj.*
   extremely dirty

3. **potent**
   (pō′ tənt) *adj.*
   powerful

4. **tattered**
   (tat′ ərd) *adj.*
   torn in shreds

5. **tangible**
   (tan′ jə bəl) *adj.*
   able to be touched

6. **sketchy**
   (skech′ ē) *adj.*
   not complete

7. **hideous**
   (hid′ ē əs) *adj.*
   very ugly; horrible

8. **deteriorate**
   (di tîr′ ē ə rāt′) *v.*
   to get worse

9. **fatigue**
   (fə tēg′) *n.*
   exhaustion

10. **clammy**
    (klam′ ē) *adj.*
    cold and damp

States of Being

1   **Word Meanings**

Opposite Meanings

 Decide which vocabulary word means the opposite of the boldfaced word or words in the sentences below. Write the correct vocabulary word in the blank.

1. Maria could not buy the art supplies because the plans were still **complete.** _____

2. The monster in the movie was so **gorgeous** that the girls covered their eyes. _____

3. The dogs were **spotless** from head to tail after rolling in the mud.
   _____

4. The patient's health was beginning to **improve** rapidly.
   _____

5. The police could not catch the **ever-present** criminal.
   _____

6. A person who perspires a lot might have **dry** hands.
   _____

7. The promising new medication has proven to be the most **ineffective** yet. _____

8. After the battle, the soldier's uniform was dirty and **in one piece.**
   _____

9. My baby sister shows signs of **alertness** by crying and rubbing her eyes. _____

10. Ideas and feelings are not **untouchable.** _____

② Reference Skills

Multiple Meanings

Read the following dictionary entries. Then write the word that correctly completes each sentence below, including the number of the definition you used.

---

fatigue *n.* **1.** a loss of strength that is caused by hard work or mental effort; weariness; exhaustion. **2.** the cause of such weariness; toil; exertion. **3.** manual labor done by military personnel. **4. fatigues** a work uniform worn by military personnel.

tattered *adj.* **1.** torn in shreds; ragged: *tattered clothing.* **2.** wearing ragged clothing: *a tattered panhandler.*

filthy *adj.* **1.** covered with or containing dirt: *filthy streets.* **2.** offensive; obscene. **3.** highly unpleasant or objectionable: *a filthy lie.*

---

1. The troops raised the _____ flag after the long, hard battle.

2. After being splashed by a car, Deena's clothes were

   _____ .

3. Athena was given _____ when she joined the army.

4. The _____ scarecrow was dressed in the farmer's old overalls that had split at the seams.

5. Ali's _____ made him sleep for 12 straight hours.

6. Compact discs that contain _____ lyrics have parental advisories.

• •

Think About It

If you are not sure which definition to choose, read the example sentence or phrase provided with the definition. Examples are included to help your understand the meaning of the word.

Vocabulary List

1. elusive

2. filthy

3. potent

4. tattered

5. tangible

6. sketchy

7. hideous

8. deteriorate

9. fatigue

10. clammy

3 Build New Vocabulary

Affixes

 Combine each word and affix below to form a new word. Then write the new word in the blank. Use a dictionary to check the spelling of each new word.

Vocabulary Word + *Affix*	New Word	Definition
1. potent + *-ial*	_____	showing of promise
2. deteriorate + *-tion*	_____	worsening
3. elusive + *-ness*	_____	inability to catch
4. *in-* + tangible	_____	not touchable
5. *im-* + potent	_____	powerless
6. hideous + *-ness*	_____	horror

• •

Write the new word you formed from the chart above that best fits in each sentence below.

7. Maya has the _____ to be a great violinist.

8. As the years passed, the streets and sidewalks showed more and more

   _____ .

9. Dreams are _____ .

10. The soldiers returned from battle, unable to erase the

    _____ of war from their minds.

11. The _____ of a criminal can make it difficult to solve a crime.

12. A wounded deer in the forest is _____ against larger animals.

 **4** **Word Play**

Similes

 Study each simile below. Write the vocabulary word that is a synonym.

Simile	**Synonym**
1. as strong as an ox	_____
2. as slippery as an eel	_____
3. as solid as a rock	_____
4. as dirty as a pig sty	_____
5. as damp as a wet sponge	_____

 Circle the word in parentheses that completes each simile below. (**Hint**: The similes below are antonyms for the similes above.)

6. as weak as a *(flea/bulldog)*

7. as sticky as *(sandpaper/glue)*

8. as untouchable as a *(soccer ball/cloud)*

9. as clean as a *(shiny penny/greasy engine)*

10. as dry as the *(desert/sun)*

1. **stroll**
   (strōl) *v.*
   to walk unhurriedly

2. **maneuver**
   (mə nŏō′ vər) *v.*
   to move through
   skillfully

3. **bound**
   (bound) *v.*
   to leap

4. **lurch**
   (lûrch) *n.*
   sudden sideways
   movement

5. **twine**
   (twīn) *v.*
   to twist around

6. **congregate**
   (kong′ gri gāt′) *v.*
   to assemble

7. **circulate**
   (sûr′ kyə lāt′) *v.*
   to move freely;
   to move in a circular
   course

8. **trudge**
   (truj) *v.*
   to walk slowly
   and wearily

9. **hover**
   (huv′ ər) *v.*
   to remain suspended;
   linger

10. **mobilize**
    (mō′ bə līz′) *v.*
    to become organized

Vocabulary for Movement

1 Word Meanings

Reading for Meaning

 Read the following passage. Look for clues to help you determine which vocabulary word fits in each blank. Write the correct word in the blank. You may need to change the form of the word so it makes sense in the sentence. Each word is used once.

Volleyball Emergency at the Beach

After checking into our hotel room, my parents and I decided to take a

break and **(1)** _____ along the beach. As we
approached the beach, we noticed a huge crowd of people

(2) _____ at the far end. We wondered why so
many people were gathered together in one place. As we carefully

(3) _____ our way through the crowd—having to

(4) _____ over people and chairs—we came upon
the reason for all the activity. We saw that a beach volleyball tournament

was about to start. Vendors were **(5)** _____
through the swarm of people, selling snacks and cold drinks. Women at

booths were showing people how to **(6)** _____
leather strings together to make necklaces. We stopped to watch the
volleyball game for a moment. Just when I thought there was no way a
player was going to reach the ball, he would lunge for it and send it flying

over the net. Wanting to see more, I **(7)** _____
through the thick sand to the bleachers. Suddenly, two players ran right
into each other and fell flat on their backs. The one in the blue shorts got

up with a **(8)** _____ and then tried to help his

teammate. By now, people were **(9)** _____ over
the man on the ground, and the paramedics began to

(10) _____, getting ready to perform any necessary
emergency medical procedures. Finally, the man got up, and the fans
cheered.

② Reference Skills

Multiple Meanings

 Read the following dictionary entries. Then write the word, or the form of the word, that correctly completes each sentence, its part of speech, and the number of its definition.

---

hover *v.* **1.** to remain hanging in the air over a certain area: *The hummingbird hovered over the flower.* **2.** to remain or linger nearby: *A small group of people hovered near the burning house.* **3.** to waver between two different states: *hover between anger and calm.*

maneuver *n.* **1.** a planned movement of military ships or troops. **2. maneuvers** training of military personnel under combat conditions: *Company B took part in manuevers with Company A.* **3.** any clever plan or action: *governmental maneuvers.* *v.* **1.** to cause (troops or vehicles) to perform a military movement: *maneuver the ships.* **2.** to move well: *maneuver one's way through the forest.* **3.** to perform a maneuver: *The ships maneuvered in the Pacific.* **4.** to employ clever moves or schemes: *She knew how to maneuver well.*

1. A large helicopter _____ over the battlefield to rescue wounded troops.

_____

2. At basic-training camp, troops took part in _____ that would help prepare them for battle.

_____

3. President Roosevelt knew how to _____ his way around obstacles to win the war.

_____

4. The American people _____ between sorrow at losing so many troops and happiness at winning the war.

_____

Vocabulary List

1. stroll
2. maneuver
3. bound
4. lurch
5. twine
6. congregate
7. circulate
8. trudge
9. hover
10. mobilize

Context Clues

Fill in each blank with the correct vocabulary word to complete the story. Change the form of the word to fit the meaning of the sentence as indicated in parentheses below each blank. Use a dictionary if you need help.

Battling the Concert-Going Crowd

The _____ of students anxiously waited to get
(+ -ion)

into the concert. Boys and girls _____ around
(+ -ed)

the crowd to try to find their friends, but it was difficult to

_____ without having to

_____ over the people sitting on the ground. Many

students were pushing to get to the front of the line and causing others

to _____ and lose their balance. No one was going

to _____ through the crowd tonight; in fact,

_____ would be the only way people could get
(+ -ing)

through.

A huge sign _____ over the main door to the
(+ -ed)

building. When the sign lit up, the ticket takers had to begin their

_____ to let fans enter. As the fans entered the
(+ -ion)

building, the ticket takers _____ wristbands
(+ -ed)

around the fans' wrists.

4 Word Play

Animal Movements

Complete each sentence below by writing the vocabulary word or the word form of the vocabulary word that best fits.

1. The kangaroo _____ over the rock.

2. The rooster _____ throughout the flock of chickens.

3. The birds began to _____ for their trip to the south.

4. The vulture _____ over the injured animal.

5. While he was walking along the branch, the monkey

   _____ but quickly recovered his balance.

6. Bats are known for _____ in large numbers—sometimes by the thousands—in places such as old barns and caves.

7. Boa constrictors like to _____ their bodies around their prey and suffocate them.

8. The sloth—a large, slow animal—_____ up the hill.

9. We saw a man and three beagles _____ happily along the path.

10. Seals can _____ themselves much more easily in the water than on land.

• •

 Think About It

If you are not familiar with one of the animals in the sentences above, look it up in an encyclopedia to learn more about it.

1. **verdict**
   (vûr´ dikt) *n.*
   jury's decision

2. **delinquent**
   (di ling´ kwənt) *adj.*
   failing in duty

3. **qualify**
   (kwol´ ə fī´) *v.*
   to meet the
   requirements

4. **ratification**
   (rat´ ə fi kā´ shən) *n.*
   official approval

5. **civics**
   (siv´ iks) *n.*
   study of duties
   of citizens and
   government

6. **ordinance**
   (or´ də nəns) *n.*
   city or town law

7. **compulsory**
   (kəm pul´ sə rē) *adj.*
   required

8. **penalize**
   (pen´ ə līz´) *v.*
   to punish

9. **circumstance**
   (sûr´ kəm stans´) *n.*
   a state or condition
   arising from an event

10. **self-evident**
    (self´ ev´ i dənt) *adj.*
    obvious; needing
    no proof

Vocabulary for Law

1 Word Meanings

Definitions

 Circle the correct short definition of each boldfaced vocabulary word below. Use a dictionary if you need help.

1. A short definition of **self-evident** is:
   a. unclear   b. obvious   c. not obvious

2. A short definition of **verdict** is:
   a. a lawyer's decision   b. a judge's decision   c. a jury's decision

3. A short definition of **circumstance** is:
   a. condition   b. reason   c. problem

4. A short definition of **delinquent** is:
   a. failing a test   b. failing in a duty   c. failing a friend

5. A short definition of **penalize** is:
   a. punish   b. reward   c. postpone

6. A short definition of **qualify** is:
   a. to exceed   b. to fall below   c. to meet

7. A short definition of **compulsory** is:
   a. free   b. required   c. unknown

8. A short definition of **ratification** is:
   a. official approval   b. unofficial approval   c. parental approval

9. A short definition of **ordinance** is:
   a. city law   b. state law   c. school law

10. A short definition of **civics** is:
    a. study of people   b. study of duties of citizens and government   c. study of nature

 Think About It

Some of the short definitions above may be synonyms. Refer to a thesaurus if a dictionary is not helpful.

② Reference Skills

Electronic Thesaurus

 Read each set of electronic thesaurus and shortened dictionary entries below. Then complete each sentence with the word from the dictionary entry that best fits.

Electronic Thesaurus

Word looked up: compulsory

Meaning: required *(adj.)*   **Synonyms:** mandatory, imperative

Dictionary

mandatory *adj.* required by law; officially ordered: *mandatory seat belts*

imperative *adj.* urgent; absolutely necessary: *It is imperative that we send help now.*

1. Although the government did not make keeping your own garden

   _____ during World War II, many people did
   so on their own to help the war effort.

2. With most young men gone to war, it was _____
   that women take jobs in factories to keep producing essential war
   equipment.

Electronic Thesaurus

Word looked up: qualify

Meanings: fit *(v.)*; limit *(v.)*   **Synonyms:** suit, restrict

suit *v.* to meet the requirements of: *He bought clothes that suited his taste.*

restrict *v.* to keep within certain boundaries; confine: to *restrict the dog to the yard*

3. Most members of the Constitutional Convention wanted to

   _____ the powers of the three branches of
   government so that no branch would be stronger than the others.

4. After 16 weeks, the members of the Constitutional Convention finally

   agreed on a constitution that best _____ the
   needs of the states and the country as a whole.

Vocabulary List

1. verdict

2. delinquent

3. qualify

4. ratification

5. civics

6. ordinance

7. compulsory

8. penalize

9. circumstance

10. self-evident

 3 **Build New Vocabulary**

Word Maps

Complete each word map below. First write the vocabulary word that belongs in the center box, and then correctly label each box *Synonym* or *Antonym*.

Word Map 1

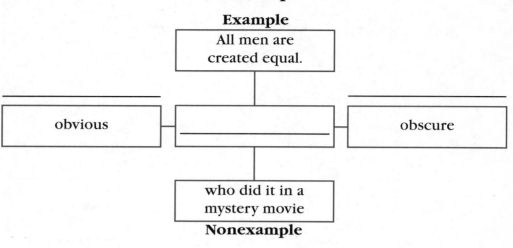

Example

All men are created equal.

_____   _____

obvious   _____   obscure

who did it in a mystery movie

Nonexample

Word Map 2

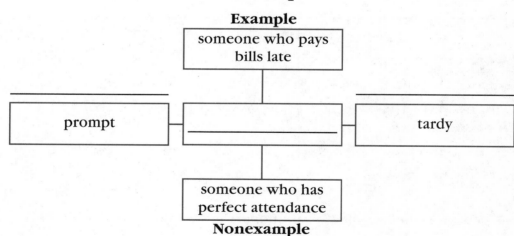

Example

someone who pays bills late

_____   _____

prompt   _____   tardy

someone who has perfect attendance

Nonexample

Word Play

Analogies

Study the relationships between the words in each analogy below. Then write the vocabulary word that completes the analogy so that the relationship in the second pair of words is the same as the one in the pair of words provided.

1. **Jury** is to _____ as **judge** is to **sentence.**

2. **Prison** is to _____ as **winner's circle** is to **reward.**

3. _____ is to **approval** as **donation** is to **gift.**

4. _____ is to **law** as **contract** is to **agreement.**

5. **Condition** is to _____ as **place** is to **site.**

6. **Hidden** is to _____ as **filthy** is to **clean.**

7. **Necessary** is to _____ as **unlawful** is to **illegal.**

8. _____ is to **restrict** as **remain** is to **stay.**

9. **Social studies** is to _____ as **biology** is to **science.**

10. _____ is to **early** as **outgoing** is to **shy.**

 ## Think About It

If you do not know the meaning of a word used in an analogy, look up the word in a dictionary. This will help you figure out the relationship between the words.

Vocabulary Review

① Review Word Meanings

Read the passage below. Then answer the questions about the boldfaced vocabulary words.

Mahatma Gandhi—Early Life

Mahatma Gandhi is known throughout the world for his quest to do away with **oppressive** laws and customs in his native land of India and in South Africa. In addition, he was largely responsible for the **liberation** of India from Great Britain. Born Mohandas Gandhi in 1869, Gandhi learned early on that nonviolent resistance could change unreasonable practices.

During the first years of his marriage, for example, his wife Kasturbai refused to **conform** to his idea of what a wife should be—very obedient and timid. Her nonviolent persuasion helped him see that there was no **justification** for how he treated her, and he changed his ways. He was married at age 13, but later in his life, he **rejected** the tradition of child marriage. He studied law in London and, once he was **qualified,** returned home to set up a practice. However, he was nervous speaking in public—trembling a little, and constantly wiping his **clammy** hands. But a business trip to South Africa would **coax** the nervousness right out of him.

Now read the following questions. Then completely fill in the bubble of the correct answer.

1. When he had to speak in public, Ghandi's hands would get ———.
   Ⓐ clammy
   Ⓑ cold
   Ⓒ swollen

2. Ghandi first had to be ——— before he could practice law.
   Ⓐ rejected
   Ⓑ coaxed
   Ⓒ qualified

3. According to the passage, what is the definition of *conform?*
   Ⓐ listen carefully
   Ⓑ behave in agreement with something
   Ⓒ use up

4. Which group of words are all synonyms for *oppressive?*
   Ⓐ fair, honest, honorable
   Ⓑ difficult, tyrannical, gloomy
   Ⓒ dirty, muddy, unclean

5. Which word is a synonym for *liberation?*
   Ⓐ release
   Ⓑ imprisonment
   Ⓒ referral

6. According to the passage, what is the definition of *justification?*
   Ⓐ a unbelievable reason
   Ⓑ a unsatisfactory reason
   Ⓒ a satisfactory reason

7. Which of the following is an example of *rejection?*
   Ⓐ a promotion
   Ⓑ a "no thank you" in response to a request for a date
   Ⓒ a birthday gift

8. In which sentence is *coax* correctly used?
   Ⓐ Because the boy was shy, his parents had to coax him to play with the other children.
   Ⓑ Did you play a coax on your friend?
   Ⓒ Do not coax the fresh paint.

Score ——— (Top Score 8)   Vocabulary Review

② Review Word Meanings

Read the passage below. Then answer the questions about the boldfaced vocabulary words.

Suffering in South Africa

On his first train ride in South Africa, Gandhi was rudely introduced to **discrimination.** He was forced from his first-class compartment and then beaten when he **rebelled** against a stagecoach driver who tried to make him sit outside of the carriage. These experiences caused Gandhi to begin his **unrelenting** fight for Indians' equal rights in South Africa. He was transformed from a nervous public speaker into an **assertive** leader for the Indian cause.

For 20 years, Gandhi used nonviolent protests to fight anti-Indian laws and **ordinances** believing that it was his moral and **civic** duty. One new law made it **compulsory** for any Indian over eight years old to register with the government and carry a special pass wherever he or she went. Gandhi **denounced** the new law and led the Indians in resisting the law nonviolently. On one occasion, he led a **congregation** of Indians in a public burning of their registration certificates. He was **penalized** time and again, serving time in jail. However, as a result of his efforts, the laws were eventually changed.

Now read the following questions. Then completely fill in the bubble of the correct answer.

1. In which sentence is *rebel* used as the same part of speech it is used as in the passage?
   - Ⓐ Rebel forces took over the city.
   - Ⓑ The Rebels of the South fought the Union soldiers during the Civil War.
   - Ⓒ Sometimes teenagers rebel against their parents.

2. Which of the following is the definition of *congregation?*
   - Ⓐ a large, out-of-control fire
   - Ⓑ the act of coming together
   - Ⓒ separation

3. What is the noun form of *civic?*
   - Ⓐ civicment
   - Ⓑ civican
   - Ⓒ civics

4. Ghandi used nonviolent protests to fight anti-Indian laws and ordinances.
   - Ⓐ True
   - Ⓑ False

5. Which pair of words could be used as synonyms for *penalized?*
   - Ⓐ thought, contemplated
   - Ⓑ contained, held
   - Ⓒ punished, disciplined

6. Which word in the passage means "bold and forward"?
   - Ⓐ discrimination
   - Ⓑ compulsory
   - Ⓒ assertive

7. According to the passage, what is the definition of *denounce?*
   - Ⓐ to speak against publicly
   - Ⓑ to give up
   - Ⓒ to reduce

8. Which sentence would be correct in a dictionary entry for *unrelenting?*
   - Ⓐ The U.S. president faces unrelenting pressure every day.
   - Ⓑ The children were unrelenting the dog from his cage.
   - Ⓒ The sound of the tide and warm tropical breeze were unrelenting.

③ Review Word Meanings

Read the passage below. Then answer the questions about the boldfaced vocabulary words.

Back to India

Proclaimed a hero in India, Gandhi returned to his native land in 1915. He turned his attention to helping Indians who were in the worst **circumstances**—the "Untouchables." Thought to be below even the lowest of the Hindu social classes, the Untouchables **underwent** terrible treatment. Untouchables were given the **filthiest** jobs and often wore **tattered** clothing and lived in poverty. Gandhi renamed the Untouchables, calling them *Harijans,* in order to help boost their self-esteem.

Gandhi also continued to work for Indian independence. On April 13, the British Army **mobilized** and **maneuvered** into position at Amritsar, where some 15,000 people had gathered to demonstrate peacefully. Some 400 men, women, and children perished that day due to the brutality of the British soldiers. Gandhi could not believe the **audacity** of the British Army, and relations with the British Empire **deteriorated.**

Now read the following questions. Then completely fill in the bubble of the correct answer.

1. The Untouchables _____ terrible treatment.
   Ⓐ undergoes
   Ⓑ undergoed
   Ⓒ underwent

2. After 400 people perished, relations between India and the British Empire _____ .
   Ⓐ maneuvered
   Ⓑ mobilized
   Ⓒ deteriorated

3. In the passage, which word could be used as a synonym for *maneuvered?*
   Ⓐ nagivated
   Ⓑ jumped
   Ⓒ rushed

4. In the passage, who was proclaimed a hero of India?
   Ⓐ the British Empire
   Ⓑ Ghandi
   Ⓒ the Harijans

5. What is an antonym for *filthy?*
   Ⓐ dirty
   Ⓑ happy
   Ⓒ clean

6. Which pair of words are synonyms for *audacity?*
   Ⓐ town, village
   Ⓑ boldness, daringness
   Ⓒ group, people

7. Which is an example of someone who is dressed in *tattered* clothing?
   Ⓐ a British soldier
   Ⓑ the Untouchables
   Ⓒ Ghandi

8. Which group of words are synonyms for *circumstance, deteriorate,* and *proclaim,* in that order?
   Ⓐ situation, decline, announce
   Ⓑ situation, decline, blame
   Ⓒ place, decline, announce

4 Review Word Meanings

Read the passage below. Then answer the questions about the boldfaced vocabulary words.

Gandhi the Leader

Gandhi, always a **potent** leader, became president of the All-India Home League, and, later, The Indian National Congress. To him, India's right to rule itself was **self-evident.** He **circulated** among the people, launching a huge program of noncooperation. He **reckoned** that the best way to make his point was through nonviolent campaigns because he believed that violence could never solve a conflict; it would only cause more trouble. He encouraged Indians not to buy British-made goods and was put on trial for causing trouble and **contradicting** British law. In response to these accusations, he **retorted** that he was innocent. But a **verdict** of guilty was given, and Gandhi was imprisoned for two years.

Throughout his life, Gandhi fasted to protest injustice and is often pictured looking very slim, as though he suffered from **fatigue.** Gandhi's decades of efforts produced lasting, **tangible** results, even after his tragic death in 1948, when he was assassinated.

Now read the following questions. Then completely fill in the bubble of the correct answer.

1. Which group of people is most often associated with the word *verdict?*
   - Ⓐ members of a musical band
   - Ⓑ a jury
   - Ⓒ reporters at a press conference

2. Which word is a synonym for *contradict?*
   - Ⓐ agree
   - Ⓑ push
   - Ⓒ deny

3. Which statement below is *self-evident,* based on what you have read about Gandhi?
   - Ⓐ Gandhi believed in bringing about change through nonviolent actions.
   - Ⓑ Gandhi was a violent, peace-hating man.
   - Ⓒ Gandhi's parents were not Indians.

4. Which of the following is *not* an example of something that is *potent?*
   - Ⓐ a tornado
   - Ⓑ a superhero
   - Ⓒ a mouse

5. Which sentence would be correct in a dictionary entry for *tangible?*
   - Ⓐ Gandhi did not want to buy a tangible.
   - Ⓑ Gandhi went off on a tangible.
   - Ⓒ Gandhi's efforts produced tangible results.

6. In response to the accusations, Gandhi _____ that he was innocent.
   - Ⓐ retorted
   - Ⓑ contradicted
   - Ⓒ circulated

7. In the passage, which word is a synonym for *reckon?*
   - Ⓐ avenge
   - Ⓑ consider
   - Ⓒ destroy

8. Which of the following is an example of something that *circulates?*
   - Ⓐ blood in the body
   - Ⓑ a television show
   - Ⓒ a dictionary

1. **melodious**
(mə lō′ dē əs) *adj.*
pleasant sounding;
musical

2. **monotonous**
(mə not′ ə nəs) *adj.*
unchanging

3. **audition**
(ô dish′ ən) *v.*
to try out for a role
in a performance

4. **chant**
(chant) *n.*
singing of words
over and over

5. **unison**
(ū′ nə sən) *n.*
sameness of pitch

6. **lyrics**
(lir′ iks) *n.*
words in a song

7. **symphony**
(sim′ fə nē) *n.*
musical composition

8. **conductor**
(kən duk′ tər) *n.*
music director

9. **discipline**
(dis′ ə plin) *n.*
training

10. **opera**
(op′ ər ə) *n.*
musical drama

Beyond the Notes

1 **Word Meanings**

Examples

  Study this lesson's Vocabulary List. Choose the correct vocabulary word to complete each sentence and write it in the blank. Refer to a dictionary if you come across an unknown word.

1. One of the greatest _____ ever created is *Otello,* a brilliant musical drama by the great composer Giuseppe Verdi.

2. Verdi's works are well loved because they are so

   _____ and pleasing to the ear.

3. The words of a pop song are called _____, and the text of an opera is called the *libretto.*

4. A great American _____, Leonard Bernstein knew how to get the most out of the orchestra he was leading.

5. A _____ might be sung to stress the importance of a word or phrase.

6. Native Americans in Mexico played rich, varied music that was

   anything but _____.

7. Choirs often sing in _____, or on the same musical note.

8. A _____, or musical composition, usually has four contrasting sections called movements.

9. The violinist Midori showed great _____ as a young girl by practicing many hours and performing for many different audiences.

10. Dorothy DeLay, a violin teacher at the Juilliard School of Music, heard

   violinists _____, or try out, to get into the school.

② Reference Skills

Multiple Meanings

Read the sample dictionary entry for *discipline*. Then answer the questions that follow.

discipline *n.* **1.** training that shapes or perfects something, such as the mind or character: *The swimmer's discipline prepared her for the Olympics.* **2.** orderly or restrained behavior; self-control: *The dieter showed great discipline when he refused a jelly doughnut.* **3.** punishment given to correct: *The parents decided that the discipline this time should be light.* **4.** a field of study: *Philosophy is an interesting discipline.* **5.** rules of conduct: *Marines at boot camp observe strict discipline.* —*v.* **1.** to teach to be obedient; keep in order and under control: *to discipline the soldiers.* **2.** to punish

1. Which part of speech is listed first? _____

2. How many noun definitions are given for *discipline?* _____

3. How many adjective definitions are given for *discipline?*

   _____

4. How many verb definitions are given for *discipline?* _____

• •

Write the correct definition of *discipline* on the line, based on the context of each sentence.

5. The drill sergeant **disciplined** the lazy recruit by ordering him to do

   fifty push-ups. _____

6. Seeing-eye dogs are **disciplined** with the utmost care so that they

   can help the blind. _____

7. Few people have the **discipline** to pass up a delicious dessert.

   _____

8. Albert Einstein's favorite **discipline** was, in all probability, physics.

   _____

Vocabulary List

1. *melodious*

2. *monotonous*

3. *audition*

4. *chant*

5. *unison*

6. *lyrics*

7. *symphony*

8. *conductor*

9. *discipline*

10. *opera*

 3 Build New Vocabulary

Word Parts

Read the word parts and their meanings below. Then use these parts to make new words, as shown. Look up each new word in the dictionary to check your answer.

symphony: *sym-* or *syn-* (together, at the same time); *-phone* (sound)

1. *syn-* + *chronos* (time) = at the same time _____

2. *phone* + *-logy* (science of) = science of speech sound

_____

monotonous: *mono-* (single; alone; one) + *-tone* (tone)

3. *mono-* + *-logue* (speak) = part for one actor speaking alone

_____

4. *mono-* + *-lith* (stone) = single big stone _____

audition: *aud-* (hear; hearing) + *-tion* (act or process)

5. *aud-* + *-torium* (room) = room where an audience sits

_____

6. *aud-* + *-ible* (able) = able to be heard _____

unison: *uni-* (one) + *-son* (sound)

7. *uni-* + *-fy* (to make, form into) = to make one

_____

8. *uni-* + *-cycle* = vehicle pushed by pedals and having one wheel

_____

 **Word Play**

Riddles and Clues

Write the word from the Vocabulary List that best fits each riddle or clue below.

1. I use a baton but I am not in a marching band. I have an ear for music, and all eyes in the orchestra are on me. Who am I?

   _____

2. You might use it on unruly children or a teenager who stayed out too late. What is it? _____

3. "Oh beautiful for spacious skies," "For amber waves of grain," and "For purple mountain majesties"—what are they?

   _____

4. I have four movements that all work together to make beautiful music. What am I? _____

5. The characters in *Hansel and Gretel, Carmen,* and *Madame Butterfly* wear lavish costumes, sing their words, and are accompanied by an orchestra. What are they performing in? _____

6. This word describes a catchy tune, a songbird's song, or a good storyteller's voice. What is it? _____

7. This phrase describes how synchronized swimmers, an ice-skating pair, and cheerleaders often perform. What is it?

   _____

8. De-fense! De-fense! De-fense! De-fense! De-fense! De-fense! What is it?

   _____

9. Most actors have to do this before they are given a role. What is it?

   _____

10. A speaker who uses only one tone of voice and speaks for hours is this. _____

1. **dawdle**
(dô´ dəl) *v.*
waste time

2. **flux**
(fluks) *n.*
constant change or movement

3. **gnarled**
(närld) *adj.*
twisted in knots

4. **gruff**
(gruf) *adj.*
harsh or hoarse, as a voice

5. **flit**
(flit) *v.*
to dart about

6. **blurt**
(blûrt) *v.*
to say suddenly

7. **garb**
(gärb) *n.*
clothing

8. **quibble**
(kwib´ əl) *v.*
to argue

9. **whim**
(hwim) *n.*
sudden or unexpected desire

10. **putter**
(put´ ər) *n.*
a golf club

Funny-Sounding Vocabulary

 Word Meanings

Analogies

 Read each analogy and figure out which vocabulary word belongs in the blank.

1. shirt is to _____
as necklace is to jewelry

2. _____ is to desire
as happy is to glad

3. _____ is to golf
as racquet is to tennis

4. _____ is to say suddenly
as scream is to yell

5. agree is to _____
as smile is to frown

6. wrinkled is to creases

as _____ is to knots

7. change is to _____
as remain is to stay

8. _____ is to happy
as nice is to grumpy

9. _____ is to waste time
as hurry is to rush

10. _____ is to stand still
as run is to walk

● ●

Think About It

If you are not familiar with a word used in an analogy, look it up in a dictionary.

② Reference Skills

Multiple Meanings

 Read the dictionary entries for each word. Then fill in each blank with the correct word and write the number and part of speech of the definition you used in the box.

putter *v.* **1.** to work or act in an aimless or useless way **2.** to waste time. — *n.* **1.** a golf club with a short shaft and an upright head. **2.** a person who putts (generally associated with golf)

gruff *adj.* **1.** deep and rough or hoarse (voice): *His gruff voice commanded respect.* **2.** abrupt, stern, or rude

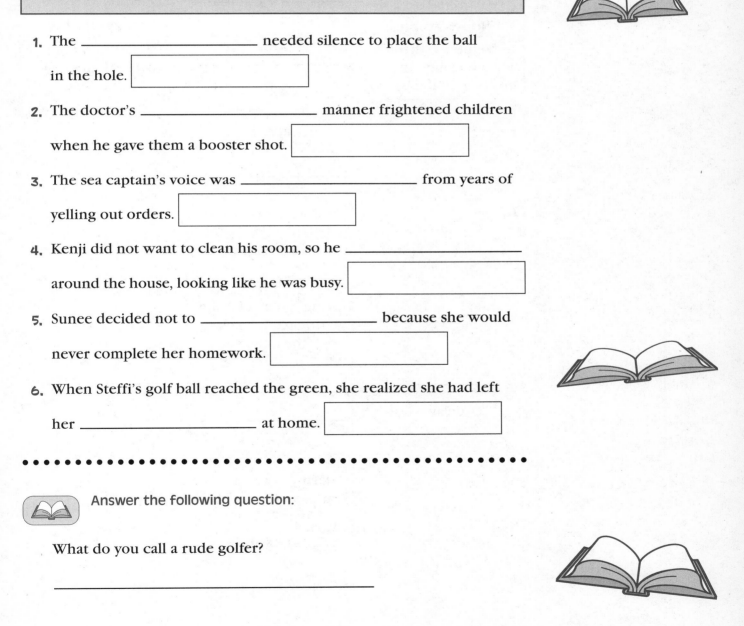

1. The _____ needed silence to place the ball

   in the hole.

2. The doctor's _____ manner frightened children

   when he gave them a booster shot.

3. The sea captain's voice was _____ from years of

   yelling out orders.

4. Kenji did not want to clean his room, so he _____

   around the house, looking like he was busy.

5. Sunee decided not to _____ because she would

   never complete her homework.

6. When Steffi's golf ball reached the green, she realized she had left

   her _____ at home.

⋯⋯⋯⋯⋯⋯⋯⋯⋯⋯⋯⋯⋯⋯⋯⋯⋯⋯

Answer the following question:

What do you call a rude golfer?

_____

Vocabulary List

1. dawdle

2. flux

3. gnarled

4. gruff

5. flit

6. blurt

7. garb

8. quibble

9. whim

10. putter

③ Build New Vocabulary

Word Maps

Complete each word map below. Fill in the middle box with the appropriate vocabulary word. Label which boxes are synonyms and which are antonyms of the vocabulary words.

Word Map I

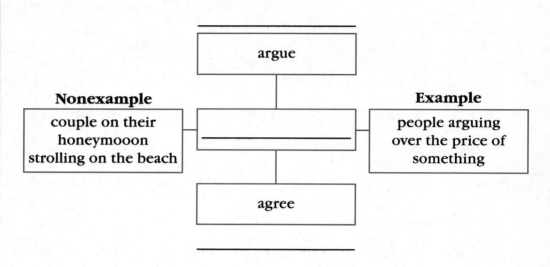

Nonexample
couple on their honeymooon strolling on the beach

argue

Example
people arguing over the price of something

agree

Word Map II

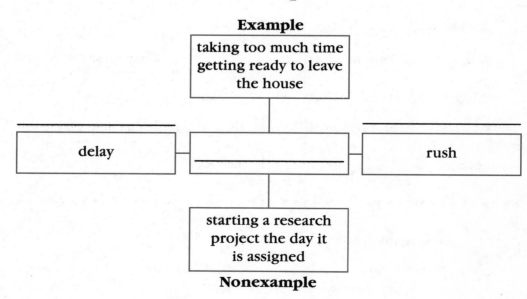

Example
taking too much time getting ready to leave the house

delay

rush

starting a research project the day it is assigned

Nonexample

 **Word Play**

Idioms

 Fill in the blanks with the word from the Vocabulary List that best fits in each sentence. If you are unsure of the meaning of any idioms, look up keywords in the dictionary or an idiom dictionary.

1. If you **twiddle your thumbs,** you are probably doing this.

   _____

2. Someone who **gets up on the wrong side of the bed** is this.

   _____

3. That man on the bench who is **as old as the hills** has hands that

   look like this. _____

4. People who are **hot under the collar** might do this over the littlest

   thing. _____

5. My brother, who tried to **bite his tongue** but instead **spilled the**

   beans, did this. _____

6. People who **change horses in the middle of the stream** are in a

   state of this. _____

7. Someone who does something **on the spur of the moment** does it

   on this. _____

8. Someone who is **out and about** does this from one location to

   another. _____

• •

 Think About It

Can you think of any other idioms that relate to a vocabulary word?

Vocabulary List

1. **lunatic**
   (lōō′ nə tik) *n.*
   insane person

2. **frenzy**
   (fren′ zē) *n.*
   outburst of
   great excitement

3. **flail**
   (flāl) *v.*
   to wave or
   swing violently

4. **barbaric**
   (bär bar′ ik) *adj.*
   uncivilized; savage

5. **monsoon**
   (mon sōōn′) *n.*
   seasonal wind of
   the Indian Ocean

6. **scandalous**
   (skan′ də ləs) *adj.*
   shocking; disgraceful

7. **torrent**
   (tor′ ənt) *n.*
   violent stream
   or downpour

8. **turbulent**
   (tûr′ byə lənt) *adj.*
   agitated; of or
   causing disorder

9. **commotion**
   (kə mō′ shən) *n.*
   noisy disturbance

10. **calamity**
    (kə lam′ i tē) *n.*
    disastrous event

"Wild" Vocabulary

1 Word Meanings

Word Choice

Study the definitions in the Vocabulary List. Then read each sentence and circle the word in parentheses that best completes the sentence.

1. The 1960s were a *(turbulent/torrent)* time for Americans—the controversy over the Vietnam War, the Civil Rights Movement, and the rising popularity of rock and roll caused much debate.

2. In the 1920s, women cut their hair short and wore short dresses—behavior that many considered to be *(calamity/scandalous)* at the time.

3. In 1993, the Mississippi River became a *(monsoon/torrent)* of disaster—leaving tens of thousands homeless.

4. The San Francisco earthquake of 1906 was a *(calamity/barbaric)* that caused more than $100 million in damage.

5. When the stock market crashed in 1929, there was a *(commotion/frenzy)* of activity at banks across the country as panicked people tried to withdraw their savings.

6. People who were mentally ill were placed in *(lunatic/barbaric)* asylums that were often poorly run and in horrible condition.

7. Some explorers thought that Native American tribes were *(scandalous/barbaric)* and called them savages.

8. Diego *(flailed/frenzied)* his arms in the air because he thought the house was on fire.

9. The rains brought by the seasonal wind known as a *(monsoon/calamity)* often last for a whole season.

10. When the enormously popular Beatles made their first trip to the United States, they caused quite a *(lunatic/commotion)*.

2 Reference Skills

Synonyms

 Read the thesaurus entries and shortened dictionary entries for the vocabulary words in the boxes below. Study the definitions and example phrases for each word, and complete the sentences with the dictionary word that best fits.

> **Thesaurus**
> **barbaric** *adj.* savage, rude, primitive
> **Dictionary**
> **rude** *adj.* not polite: *rude remark*
> **savage** *adj.* not tamed; wild: *Savage dogs guarded the junkyard.*
> **primitive** *adj.* crude or simple: *primitive tools*

1. Archaeologists have found _____ pottery, weapons, and jewelry from thousands of years ago.

2. Lions are _____ animals that kill their prey for food.

3. Hanging up the phone without saying goodbye is considered to be

   _____.

> **Thesaurus**
> **lunatic** *adj.* insane, zany, absurd
> **Dictionary**
> **insane** *adj.* mentally ill: *The jury thought the criminal was insane.*
> **zany** *adj.* funny in a silly or ridiculous way: *zany circus clowns*
> **absurd** *adj.* ridiculous; contrary to reason or good sense: *The idea that the moon is made of green cheese is absurd.*

4. The _____ comedian had the audience roaring with laughter.

5. In earlier times, some people thought the idea of space travel was

   _____.

6. Some _____ people can be helped with medication and therapy.

Vocabulary List

1. lunatic
2. frenzy
3. flail
4. barbaric
5. monsoon
6. scandalous
7. torrent
8. turbulent
9. commotion
10. calamity

 3 **Build New Vocabulary**

Word Forms

Fill in the blanks below with the correct letters. Refer to a dictionary if you are unsure of the spelling or word choice.

1. The adjective form of *scandal*   scandal___ ___ ___

2. The adjective form of *calamity*   calamit___ ___ ___

3. The adjective form of *frenzy*   frenz___ ___ ___

4. A noun form (person) of *barbaric*   barbar___ ___ ___

5. A noun form of *lunatic*   luna___ ___

6. The adjective form of *torrent*   torrent___ ___ ___

7. A noun form of *turbulent*   turbul___ ___ ___ ___

• •

Fill in the blanks below with the correct word from the exercise above.

8. There was an outbreak of _____ after the teacher left the classroom.

9. Portia had a _____ look on her face because a dog had chased her home.

10. _____ rains can make a river overflow

11. If you experience _____ on an airplane, you should fasten your seat belt.

12. The student's _____ behavior caused her to get sent to the principal's office.

13. Jaunita is a _____ girl; a disastrous event seems to follow her everywhere.

14. Khoa acted like a _____ when he chased people around the playground.

 **Word Play**

Word Origins

 Fill in the blanks with the word from the Vocabulary List that best fits.

1. The word _____ comes from the idea that the changes in the phases of the moon caused some people to become crazy.

2. The word _____ most likely comes from the Latin word *clades,* which means "destruction."

3. The word _____ comes from the Arabic word for *season* because it is something that occurs during a certain season.

4. The word _____ is related to the words *frenetic* and *frantic,* which are based on the Greek word *phrenitis,* meaning "swelling of the brain."

5. The word _____ comes from the Greek word meaning "foreign" or "ignorant."

6. The word _____ comes from the Latin word *flagellum,* which means "whip."

7. The word _____ is based on the Latin word *turba,* which means "crowd" or "confusion."

8. The word _____ comes from the Latin and Greek words that mean "trap," "stumbling block," or "offense."

9. The word _____ has the Latin root *movere,* which means "to move."

10. When you think of the word _____, you think of rain, but it comes from the Latin word for "burn."

Vocabulary List

1. **libel**
   (lī' bəl) n.
   false charge

2. **relevant**
   (rel' ə vənt) adj.
   appropriate

3. **converse**
   (kən vûrs') v.
   to discuss; talk

4. **ethical**
   (eth' i kəl) adj.
   moral

5. **principle**
   (prin' sə pəl) n.
   a basic truth or belief

6. **confidential**
   (kon' fi den' shəl) adj.
   secret; private

7. **publicity**
   (pu blis' i tē) n.
   public notice
   or attention

8. **disclose**
   (dis klōz') v.
   to make known

9. **represent**
   (rep' ri zent') v.
   stand for; symbolize

10. **slant**
    (slant) v.
    to present in a
    certain way

Reporting the News

1 Word Meanings

Synonyms

Fill in the blanks with the vocabulary words that best fit with the synonyms listed below. Look up the synonyms in the dictionary, if necessary.

1. moral, virtuous, good _____

2. advertising, marketing, promoting _____

3. misrepresentation, defamation, lie _____

4. symbolize, stand for, portray _____

5. secret, private, restricted _____

6. appropriate, fitting, suitable _____

7. discuss, talk, chat _____

8. angle, incline, distort _____

9. reveal, uncover, tell _____

10. belief, law, rule _____

② Reference Skills

Homographs

 The following sentences include homographs, which are words that have the same spelling but different meanings and, sometimes, different pronunciations. Use the brief dictionary definitions to decide which meaning best fits each sentence, and write it in the blank.

> **converse** *v.* (kən vûrs´) to talk together
>
> **converse** *adj.* (kon´ vûrs) opposite or reverse in order, action, or direction

1. Philip did the **converse** of everything his mother said.

   _____

2. Franklin Roosevelt would often **converse** with Winston Churchill, the prime minister of Great Britain, during World War II.

   _____

3. The **converse** of war is peace.

   _____

> **resume** *v.* to go on after an interruption
>
> **resume** *n.* a statement of a person's work record, used in applying for a job (also written *resumé* or *résumé*)

4. It is important to place your education on a **resume.**

   _____

5. If it is time to go home and your teacher is in the middle of a lesson, he or she will **resume** the lesson the next day.

   _____

6. On the job interview, a possible employer will ask to see a **resume.**

   _____

Vocabulary List

1. libel

2. relevant

3. converse

4. ethical

5. principle

6. confidential

7. publicity

8. disclose

9. represent

10. slant

③ Build New Vocabulary

Context Clues

 Read each sentence below. Fill in the blank with the correct word from the box.

confidentiality	libelous	relevance	conversation
representation	publicize	representative	confidentially

1. Reporters who write untrue stories make

   _____ remarks.

2. Most movies are _____ of real life.

3. Doctors promise patients _____ about their health problems.

4. Thomas Jefferson had long _____ with his fellow signers of the Declaration of Independence.

5. _____ speaking, I think I have as good a chance as any at making the basketball team.

6. An ambassador is a _____ of the United States who lives in a foreign country.

7. If a school wants to have a successful bake sale, it needs to

   _____ the event weeks before it happens.

8. Chemists try to figure out the _____ of chemical reactions.

● ●

Think About It

If you cannot find one of the words listed above in a dictionary, try looking up the vocabulary word on the list it is related to.

4 Word Play

Poetic Language

 Fill in each blank with the vocabulary word that best fits.
(**Hint:** Clues are provided in parentheses.)

Elephant Blues

The 1. _____ elephant did not think it
(**alliteration**)

2. _____ that the circus was his life.
(**near rhyme**)

To show the world his misery, He wanted

3. _____ about being forbidden to take
(**near rhyme**)

a wife. So a reporter printed his story, and the mayor asked

him, "Who do you 4. _____?
(**end rhyme**)

The one who eats insects for dinner and sleeps in a tent?"

"My dear man," he replied, "I have to

5. _____ what I have learned you
(**end rhyme**)

outwardly oppose!" "That is not true!" the mayor started to rant,

"The news that you write is written with a 6. _____!"
(**end rhyme**)

"I am proud of my 7. _____," the reporter replied.
(**consonance**)

"I report what I see—that is for me to decide." "I cannot

8. _____ with this clown anymore,"
(**alliteration**)

the mayor mumbled as he made for the door.

1. **rendezvous**
(rän´ də voō´) n.
meeting place

2. **gourmet**
(goōr mā´) n.
expert in good food
and drink

3. **petite**
(pə tēt´) adj.
small

4. **cuisine**
(kwi zēn´) n.
style of cooking

5. **cliché**
(klē shā´) n.
overused saying

6. **debris**
(də brē´) n.
remains of something
destroyed

7. **debonair**
(deb´ ə nâr´) adj.
charming and pleasant

8. **pedigree**
(ped´ i grē´) n.
line of ancestors

9. **suede**
(swād) n.
soft, velvety leather

10. **beret**
(bə rā´) n.
brimless cap

Vocabulary from French

1 Word Meanings

Definitions

After studying the short definitions for this lesson's vocabulary
words, match the vocabulary word to its complete definition.

1. ☐ beret

2. ☐ rendezvous

3. ☐ suede

4. ☐ gourmet

5. ☐ pedigree

6. ☐ petite

7. ☐ debonair

8. ☐ cuisine

9. ☐ debris

10. ☐ cliché

A. of small size; tiny; little

B. remains of something broken or
destroyed; rubbish

C. line of ancestors; descent; lineage

D. an appointment to meet at a fixed
place or time

E. a soft, round cap, usually without
a brim

F. the manner or style of cooking or
preparing food

G. a soft leather that feels like velvet

H. courteous, charming, and pleasant

I. an expression, phrase, or idea that has
lost its originality or effect because it
has been used too much

J. a person who is expert in choosing
and judging fine food and drink

 ### Think About It

Many of the words on this Vocabulary List are pronounced differently from
the way they look. Remember to look at the phonetic respelling when you
need to pronounce one of these words.

2 Reference Skills

Connotation

 Look up each pair of synonyms in the dictionary and study the definitions and example sentences. Then put a check next to the one that you think has the more *positive* connotation. If you think the connotations are the same, then check the "Same" box.

Vocabulary Word		Synonym		Same
1. rendezvous	☐	meeting	☐	☐
2. gourmet	☐	glutton	☐	☐
3. cuisine	☐	food	☐	☐
4. petite	☐	scrawny	☐	☐
5. debris	☐	garbage	☐	☐
6. debonair	☐	dashing	☐	☐
7. clichéd	☐	corny	☐	☐
8. beret	☐	cap	☐	☐

Vocabulary List

1. *rendezvous*

2. *gourmet*

3. *petite*

4. *cuisine*

5. *cliché*

6. *debris*

7. *debonair*

8. *pedigree*

9. *suede*

10. *beret*

3 Build New Vocabulary

Word Origins

Fill in the blanks with the word from the Vocabulary List that best fits.

1. The word _____ comes from the French words *de bon aire,* which mean "of good family or nature."

2. The word _____ comes from the French word *clicher,* which means "a printer's stereotype." A stereotype is a metal cast of a print that is used to print words. The word *stereotyped* today also means "unoriginal" or "ordinary."

3. *Pied de grue* means "crane's foot" in French. This is what the word

   _____ is based on, because the lines of a family tree look like a crane's foot.

4. The word _____ comes from the French phrase *gants de Suéde,* which means "gloves of Sweden," probably because the gloves were made of a soft, velvety leather.

5. The word _____ is the French word for "kitchen."

6. The word _____ is based on the French verb *debriser,* which means "to break to pieces."

7. The word _____ means "to present yourselves," especially at a meeting place.

8. The word _____ is most likely based on the Middle French word *gromet,* which means "boy servant."

• •

Think About It

What reference book would you use to determine a word's origin?

 **Word Play**

Foreign Words and Phrases

 Read the common foreign words and phrases and their meanings in the box below. Then fill in the blanks with the words that best fit each clue.

---

carpe diem (Latin) Seize the day.

C'est la vie! (French) That's life!

¡Hasta la vista! (Spanish) See you soon!

Arigatou (Japanese) Thank you

wunderbar (German) wonderful

semper fidelis (Latin) always faithful

Eureka! (Greek) I have found it!

Aloha (Hawaiian) hello or good-bye

---

1. California's motto—this is what gold rushers would say when they found gold. _____

2. "Once a marine, always a marine"—this is one saying shared among members of the United States Marine Corps. Based on this, what do you think their motto is? _____

3. If someone was going on a trip you might say this.

   _____

4. At the end of a great musical performance you might clap your hands and say this. _____

5. Get up off the couch and do something! _____

6. Something said by a person who is next in line to buy tickets when the ticket seller announces the show is sold out.

   _____

7. You would say this to someone who has given you a gift.

   _____

8. This can be used as a greeting or farewell.

   _____

Vocabulary Review

1 Review Word Meanings

Read the passage below. Then answer the questions about the boldfaced vocabulary words.

Giant of Jazz

Born Edward Kennedy Ellington in 1899, Duke Ellington became the most accomplished jazz composer of his time. Duke was born in Washington, D.C., where his mother was a homemaker and his father catered fine **cuisine.** Duke earned his nickname early on—tall, **debonair,** and well spoken, he was considered to be a "regal" young man. Although his parents played the piano, Duke's first love was baseball. Not even a **monsoon** could force him from the game. However, after a **calamity** with a baseball bat, Duke's mother convinced him to quit the sport.

After hearing a young pianist play, Duke decided on a **whim** that he would be a **lunatic** not to pursue his great gift of music. He practiced the piano and eventually assembled a great group of musicians called Duke Ellington and the Washingtonians. Their favorite **rendezvous** was Harlem, where many of the great artists were, as well as where the hubbub and **commotion** was. For the next 15 years, Duke composed a **torrent** of jazz compositions—some 2,000 in all—and Duke Ellington and His Orchestra became the first black jazz band to play Carnegie Hall.

Now read the following questions. Then completely fill in the bubble of the correct answer.

1. What is a synonym for *commotion?*
   - Ⓐ music
   - Ⓑ comedy
   - Ⓒ uproar

2. Choose a synonym for the boldfaced word, based on the following analogy:
   calm is to *peaceful* as
   lunatic is to *crazy.*
   - Ⓐ serene
   - Ⓑ sane
   - Ⓒ insane

3. Duke's father catered fine cuisine. What is the definition of *cuisine?*
   - Ⓐ culture
   - Ⓑ people
   - Ⓒ style of food

4. *Impulse* is not a synonym for *whim.*
   - Ⓐ true
   - Ⓑ false

5. What is the definition of *monsoon,* as it is used in the passage above?
   - Ⓐ seasonal wind of the Indian Ocean
   - Ⓑ heavy rainfall
   - Ⓒ earthquake

6. In which phrase is *torrent* correctly used?
   - Ⓐ a torrent of information
   - Ⓑ drinking the torrent
   - Ⓒ walking on the torrent

7. Duke earned his nickname because he was
   - Ⓐ torrent.
   - Ⓑ lunatic.
   - Ⓒ debonair.

8. In which sentence is *rendezvous* correctly used?
   - Ⓐ The Mexican restaurant was their favorite rendezvous.
   - Ⓑ The dog rendezvoused the cat.
   - Ⓒ This rendezvous is delicious.

Score _____ (Top Score 8)   Vocabulary Review

② Review Word Meanings

Read the passage below. Then answer the questions about the boldfaced vocabulary words.

First Lady of Song

Born in 1918, Ella Fitzgerald was known to her fans as the First Lady of Song. Her early life was in a state of **flux** when her father died shortly after she was born. Her mother moved them from Virginia to Yonkers, New York. She instilled **discipline** in Ella, encouraging her to nurture her love of dancing and singing. However, at her first talent show, at a Harlem **opera** house, Ella froze. She found herself unable to perform the dance routine she had planned, and hearing the **gruff** voices of hecklers in the audience, she nervously **blurted** out a song she had heard on the radio. To her surprise, she won a $25 prize.

After her first success, the sky was the limit for Ella, to use an old **cliché.** Although the years of the Depression were **turbulent,** Ella found work as a singer with a musician named Chick Webb. He and his wife Sallye took Ella under their wings, and after **conversing** with each other, decided to adopt her. Ella's first big hit was a swinging version of the nursery rhyme "A-Tiskit, A-Tasket." Adapting the rhyme into a song, she used its words as **lyrics.** Ella's voice earned her many more hits, worldwide **publicity** and fame, and more Grammy awards than any other female vocalist in history.

• •

Now read the following questions. Then completely fill in the bubble of the correct answer.

1. Which meaning of *discipline* is used in the passage above?
   Ⓐ punishment
   Ⓑ self-control
   Ⓒ a branch of knowledge

2. What is the connotation of *gruff?*
   Ⓐ positive
   Ⓑ neutral
   Ⓒ negative

3. Which meaning of *converse* is used in the passage above?
   Ⓐ discuss
   Ⓑ reversed
   Ⓒ something that is opposite of

4. Which example sentence would be correct in a dictionary entry for *blurt?*
   Ⓐ The pitcher blurted the ball to the catcher.
   Ⓑ The sheep blurted.
   Ⓒ The student blurted out the answer.

5. Which is an example of a *cliché?*
   Ⓐ The sky is the limit.
   Ⓑ Mary Had a Little Lamb
   Ⓒ *The Chronicles of Narnia*

6. Which pair of words would most likely be found in a thesaurus entry for *flux?*
   Ⓐ failure, dud
   Ⓑ change, uncertainty
   Ⓒ shine, polish

7. Which word in the passage above is a synonym for *stormy?*
   Ⓐ turbulent
   Ⓑ publicity
   Ⓒ cliché

8. What is the dictionary definition for *opera?*
   Ⓐ a trick played on the eyes
   Ⓑ a play that is sung
   Ⓒ an Italian dish

9. Which example sentence would be correct in a dictionary entry for *lyrics?*
   Ⓐ The purse cost 200 Italian lyrics.
   Ⓑ The lyrics were eaten during Medieval times.
   Ⓒ Many parents objected to the song's lyrics.

10. Which word would you find as a synonym in a thesaurus for *publicity?*
    Ⓐ common
    Ⓑ advertising
    Ⓒ television

③ Review Word Meanings

Read the passage below. Then answer the questions about the boldfaced vocabulary words.

Music Man

Born in Massachusetts in 1918, Leonard Bernstein did not have to say a word while he was in front of audiences because his music spoke for him. A **conductor** of **symphonies,** he was known to **flail** his arms about as he worked the orchestra into a **frenzy.** He composed captivating music, including **melodious** musicals such as the extremely successful *West Side Story.*

Leonard Bernstein also wrote operettas and books and hosted a television show on which different kinds of music were **represented.** Finally, he taught music courses, relating to his students what he thought was **relevant** in the world of music. Even as he got older, and his music career came to a close, he still received recognition for his work, including a Grammy Lifetime Achievement Award. Like his music, Leonard Bernstein's life was never **monotonous** and his musical efforts are still enjoyed by many fans around the world.

Now read the following questions. Then completely fill in the bubble of the correct answer.

1. If *irrelevant* means "inappropriate," then what does *relevant* mean?
   - Ⓐ not appropriate
   - Ⓑ relative
   - Ⓒ suitable

2. What is a synonym for *monotonous?*
   - Ⓐ similar
   - Ⓑ boring
   - Ⓒ changing

3. Leonard Bernstein wrote _____ musicals.
   - Ⓐ melodious
   - Ⓑ monotonous
   - Ⓒ flailing

4. If *syn-* means "together," and *phone* means "sound," then what is the main job of the members of a *symphony?*
   - Ⓐ playing together to make music
   - Ⓑ talking to each other on the phone
   - Ⓒ listening to music together

5. What does someone who *conducts* do?
   - Ⓐ leads an orchestra
   - Ⓑ acts correctly
   - Ⓒ eats a meal

6. Which pair of synonyms could replace *represent* in the passage above?
   - Ⓐ hated, disliked
   - Ⓑ depicted, described
   - Ⓒ donated, given

7. Which is the best example of someone who is known to *flail?*
   - Ⓐ a conductor
   - Ⓑ an elderly person
   - Ⓒ a student

8. Which word could not be substituted for *frenzy* in the passage above?
   - Ⓐ fury
   - Ⓑ calmness
   - Ⓒ rage

4 Review Word Meanings

Read the passage below. Then answer the questions about the boldfaced vocabulary words.

The King of Rock and Roll

Considered one of rock and roll's greatest performers, Elvis Presley began his adult life driving trucks. But his big break came when he was 18, and he did not even have to **audition.** When Elvis went to a recording studio to record songs for his mother, the manager did not **dawdle** in introducing him to the studio owner. He had his first big hit at age 21—"Heartbreak Hotel"—and before he knew it, his personal life was no longer **confidential.**

Music **journalists** wrote about every aspect of his life—from family **scandals** to the details of his **pedigree.** Elvis's fans wanted to know everything about the "King of Rock and Roll," even though they knew the stories were sometimes **slanted** to sound more exciting. At his concerts, huge crowds of fans would **chant** in **unison,** "Elvis! Elvis!" Later in his career he was known for his wild **garb,** wearing flashy sequined jackets and big sunglasses. Some of his other big hits include "All Shook Up," "Love Me Tender," and "Blue **Suede** Shoes."

Now read the following questions. Then completely fill in the bubble of the correct answer.

1. According to the passage, what is the definition of *slant?*
   - Ⓐ make up
   - Ⓑ present in a certain way
   - Ⓒ an angle

2. Elvis's life was confidential.
   - Ⓐ true
   - Ⓑ false

3. Which word is a synonym for *contradict?*
   - Ⓐ agree
   - Ⓑ push
   - Ⓒ deny

4. If *uni-* means "one," and *son* means "sound," then what are people who are talking in *unison* doing?
   - Ⓐ taking turns talking
   - Ⓑ saying the same thing at the same time
   - Ⓒ speaking loudly

5. Which of the following would you *audition* for?
   - Ⓐ a role in a play
   - Ⓑ a meal
   - Ⓒ a CD player

6. Which example sentence would be correct in a dictionary entry for *dawdle?*
   - Ⓐ The toddler dawdled the glass and it broke.
   - Ⓑ She dawdled the entire glass of milk.
   - Ⓒ The children dawdled on their way to school.

7. Which of the following is an example of *garb?*
   - Ⓐ Elvis's outfits
   - Ⓑ newspapers stories
   - Ⓒ Elvis's concerts

8. What is the definition of *suede,* based on the following analogy?
   cloth is to *cotton*
   as *leather* is to *suede*
   - Ⓐ a kind of cloth
   - Ⓑ a kind of leather
   - Ⓒ a piece of clothing

9. Which word is a synonym for *pedigree?*
   - Ⓐ doctor
   - Ⓑ descent
   - Ⓒ education

10. Which of the following is an example of something that *chants?*
    - Ⓐ a cat
    - Ⓑ a tractor
    - Ⓒ a fan

Vocabulary List

1. **foliage**
   (fō´ lē ij) *n.*
   leaves on a tree or plant

2. **erosion**
   (i rō´ zhən) *n.*
   wearing away

3. **consumer**
   (kən sōō´ mər) *n.*
   one who uses up; a buyer and a user

4. **biological**
   (bī´ ə loj´ i kəl) *adj.*
   having to do with life

5. **migrate**
   (mī´ grāt) *v.*
   to move to another region

6. **deplete**
   (di plēt´) *v.*
   to use up

7. **habitat**
   (hab´ i tat´) *n.*
   place in which plants and animals live

8. **predator**
   (pred´ ə tər) *n.*
   animal that preys on other animals

9. **scavenger**
   (skav´ ən jər) *n.*
   animal that feeds on decaying animals

10. **toxic**
    (tok´ sik) *adj.*
    poisonous

Ecology Vocabulary

1 Word Meanings

Fill-In-the-Blank

 Use the short definitions provided in the Vocabulary List to determine which vocabulary word completes each sentence. Make sure that answers follow subject-verb agreement. Write the answer in the blank.

1. Vultures are known as _____ because they feed almost entirely on animals that are dead and decaying.

2. Tigers are fierce _____, rushing and killing deer, cattle, and other animals for food about once a week.

3. The golden eagle's _____ is the mountainous areas in the western United States and Canada.

4. Many species of geese _____ south for the winter in search of a milder climate.

5. Some scientists believe that petroleum reserves will be

   _____ in the next few decades and that other sources of energy must be used instead.

6. The skin mucus of poison dart frogs is extremely

   _____, causing loss of movement or even death in predators that eat them.

7. Travelers appreciate the brilliant colors of a forest's fall

   _____.

8. In dry climates, _____ can occur because the top layer of rock might expand as a result of the heat and then crack off from the cooler rock that is under it.

9. Advertisers try to appeal to _____ who buy and use their products.

10. During recent space shuttle missions, scientists did

    _____ experiments, such as determining what kind of effect space had on frogs' eggs.

② Reference Skills

Multiple Meanings

 Read the dictionary entries for each word. Then fill in each blank with the correct form of the word and write the number of the definition you used in the box.

> **consume** *v.* **1.** to use up: *The refrigerator consumes electricity.* **2.** to eat or drink, especially in large amounts: *They consumed a five-course meal.* **3.** to destroy, as by fire: *The fire consumed the barn.* **4.** to occupy all the attention of; engross: *The crowd was consumed with anger.*
>
> **scavenger** *n.* **1.** an animal that feeds on decaying animals or plants: *The vulture is a scavenger.* **2.** a person who looks through garbage for things that can be used or sold; a junk collector: *The scavengers came out on garbage collection day.*
>
> **erode** *v.* **1.** to wear away or wash away slowly by action of water, wind, or glacier: *The shoreline slowly eroded over the years.* **2.** to cause to disappear or diminish gradually: *The relationship between the countries was eroded by disagreements over trade.*

1. Fires _____ millions of acres of forest every

   year. ☐

2. When a building is on fire, firefighters are _____

   with getting everyone out alive. ☐

3. In contrast to the spotted hyena, which fiercely attacks its prey, the

   striped hyena is mostly a _____, often eating

   bones and other remains of animals. ☐

4. Friendships are sometimes _____ by

   arguments over meaningless things. ☐

5. In some restaurants, patrons _____ more than

   five courses of food. ☐

6. High cliffs are often _____ by wind and

   rain. ☐

Vocabulary List

1. foliage
2. erosion
3. consumer
4. biological
5. migrate
6. deplete
7. habitat
8. predator
9. scavenger
10. toxic

3 Build New Vocabulary

Related Words

Select the word from the Vocabulary List that is related to the defined word. Write your answer in the blank provided.

1. **biosphere** *n.* —the part of earth—its waters and atmosphere—where life is found _____

2. **erode** *v.* —to wear away gradually by rubbing or friction

   _____

3. **toxin** *n.* —any poisonous product of animal or vegetable cells

   _____

4. **consumption** *n.* —the act of using up _____

5. **predatory** *adj.* —living by preying on other animals

   _____

6. **migrant** *n.* —a person or thing that moves from one area to another to settle there _____

7. **habitual** *adj.* —done by or resulting from doing an action that one does not have to think about _____

8. **foliation** *n.* —the act or process of putting forth leaves

   _____

• •

Think About It

Do you know any other words that are related to the words on the Vocabulary List?

 **Word Play**

Rhyming Clues

Fill in the blank with the vocabulary word that best completes the rhyme.

1. The chicken outran the fox and got ahead of 'er, that wily, hungry, clever _____.

2. "Hurry," she quacked, "Let's not be late. We don't want to be the last to _____."

3. We must drink only what is needed, for our water supply is nearly _____.

4. We heard a very nasty rumor about how the widget makers fooled the _____.

5. Did you see where that big white rabbit sat? I'm quite sure that's not its natural _____.

6. The drinking water made that ox sick. The scientists agreed it was fairly _____.

7. No, that canyon wasn't caused by an explosion; it was made by a process called _____.

8. We wanted to determine the tree's lineage, but first we had to examine the _____.

9. Out of the blue there came a challenger who claimed that they had identified the wrong _____.

10. The scientist knew the problem was not geological because he found facts that said it was _____.

Health Vocabulary

1 **Word Meanings**

Analogies

Examine the relationship between the pair of words in each item below. Choose the correct vocabulary word that completes the other part of the analogy.

1. infirmary
(in fûr′ mə rē) *n.*
place for the sick

2. quarantine
(kwor′ ən tēn′) *v.*
to keep apart
from others

3. contagious
(kən tā′ jəs) *adj.*
spread easily

4. inflammation
(in′ flə mā′ shən) *n.*
swelling of the body

5. robust
(rō bust′) *adj.*
healthy and
strong; vigorous

6. intense
(in tens′) *adj.*
of a high degree;
very great or strong

7. detrimental
(det′ rə men′ təl) *adj.*
harmful

8. revive
(ri vīv′) *v.*
to bring back to
consciousness

9. symptom
(simp′ təm) *n.*
sign of an illness

10. cardiac
(kär′ dē ak′) *adj.*
of the heart

1. _____ is to **sick**
as **school** is to **children**

2. the **sniffles** is to the **common cold**

as _____ is to **catching**

3. **calm** is to **relaxed**

as _____ is to **irritation**

4. _____ is to **harmful**
as **healthy** is to **well**

5. _____ is to **unconscious**
as **feed** is to **hungry**

6. _____ is to **sign**
as **aches** is to **pains**

7. **sick** is to **ill**

as _____ is to **isolate**

8. _____ is to **heart**
as **oral** is to **mouth**

9. **dangerous** is to **hazardous**

as _____ is to **extreme**

10. _____ is to **weak**
as **stormy** is to **calm**

2 Reference Skills

Degrees of Meaning

 Look up each pair of synonyms and study the definitions and example sentences. Each pair contains a vocabulary word from this or a previous lesson. Put a check next to the word that you think is more intense in meaning.

1. robust _____   fit _____

2. inflammation _____   irritation _____

3. fierce _____   intense _____

4. contagious _____   communicable _____

5. quarantine _____   separate _____

6. libel _____   gossip _____

7. detrimental _____   awful _____

8. restore _____   revive _____

9. flail _____   wave _____

10. infirmary _____   hospital _____

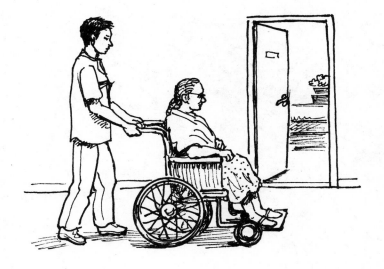

Vocabulary List

1. *infirmary*

2. *quarantine*

3. *contagious*

4. *inflammation*

5. *robust*

6. *intense*

7. *detrimental*

8. *revive*

9. *symptom*

10. *cardiac*

3 Build New Vocabulary

Word Origins

Fill in the blanks with the word from the Vocabulary List that fits best.

1. _____ comes from the Greek word *kardia,* which means "heart."

2. _____ comes from the Latin word for "forty," *quaranta,* because this was the number of days that a ship with sick people on board had to stay in port before anyone was allowed off.

3. _____ comes from the Greek word that means "fall together," because often signs of illness, such as fever and sneezing, would occur at the same time, or "fall together."

4. _____ comes from the Latin word *robur,* which means "oak" or "strength."

5. _____ comes from the Latin root *vivere,* which means "to live," and the prefix *re-,* which means "again."

6. _____ comes from the Latin word *contingere,* which means "to have contact with" or "to pollute."

7. _____ comes from the Latin word *firmus,* which means "not weak," and the prefix *in-,* which means "not."

8. _____ comes from the same Latin word as *detritus,* which means "debris" or "a product of wearing away."

 **Word Play**

Onomatopoeia

 Choose onomatopoeic sounds from the box below that best match each description.

Cock-a-doodle-doo!	Thud!	Beep, beep!
Woof!	Hee hee hee!	Ah-choo!
	thump bump	buzz

1. Someone who is in an **infirmary** might say this.

   _____

2. An example of a **cardiac** sound is this.

   _____

3. A **symptom** of hearing loss might sound like this.

   _____

4. A **robust** rooster might say this every morning.

   _____

5. A dog might do this when someone knocks **intensely** at the door.

   _____

6. Someone who needs to be **revived** might have fainted and made

   this sound. _____

7. Some people say that this is **contagious.**

   _____

8. If a driver does something that is **detrimental** to other drivers, he

   might hear this. _____

1. tart
(tärt) *adj.*
sour in taste

2. devour
(di vour´) *v.*
to eat up greedily

3. bland
(bland) *adj.*
mild in taste

4. edible
(ed´ ə bəl) *adj.*
fit to eat

5. indulge
(in dulj´) *v.*
to allow oneself to
enjoy something

6. temptation
(temp tā´ shən) *n.*
attraction

7. aroma
(ə rō´ mə) *n.*
a pleasant odor

8. luscious
(lush´ əs) *adj.*
delicious

9. pungent
(pun´ jənt) *adj.*
sharp to the taste
or smell

10. savor
(sā´ vər) *v.*
to taste or smell
with pleasure

Food Vocabulary

 Word Meanings

Synonyms

 Choose the word from the Vocabulary List that best fits with each group of synonyms listed below. Look up the synonyms in the dictionary, if necessary.

1. eatable, palatable, nutritious _____

2. gobble, swallow, consume _____

3. tangy, sharp, hot _____

4. appreciate, enjoy, like _____

5. soothing, mild, agreeable _____

6. scent, smell, fragrance _____

7. tasty, delectable, scrumptious _____

8. fascination, appeal, allure _____

9. acidic, bitter, sour _____

10. allow, permit, grant _____

Think About It

Do the synonyms listed above for each vocabulary word have the same meaning? Remember, synonyms have similar meanings and possibly different connotations.

② Reference Skills

Multiple Meanings

 Read the dictionary entries for each word. Then fill in each blank with the correct form of the word and write the number of the definition you used in the box.

> **bland** *adj.* **1.** uninteresting; lacking excitement: *a bland story.*
> **2.** soothing; not irritating: *a bland diet.* **3.** agreeable or pleasant:
> *a bland smile.*
>
> **devour** *v.* **1.** to eat up greedily: *The hungry man devoured his
> dinner.* **2.** to use up in a destructive manner: *The fire devoured
> the barn.* **3.** to enjoy greatly: *devour a book.*
>
> **tart** *adj.* **1.** sharp in taste; sour: *The grapefruit juice was tart.*
> **2.** sharp in tone; biting: *His tart remark hurt her. n.* **3.** a pastry
> shell that contains a filling: *The cherry tart tasted delicious.*

1. People who suffer from severe heartburn should stick to

   _____ foods. ☐

2. Bakeries often sell _____ with different kinds

   of filling. ☐

3. The young Theodore Roosevelt _____ books

   and articles on natural history. ☐

4. Because of his many interesting adventures, Roosevelt probably

   never told a _____ story. ☐

5. Some comedians are known for their _____

   jokes. ☐

6. The college students _____ the pizza in ten

   minutes. ☐

Vocabulary List

1. tart

2. devour

3. bland

4. edible

5. indulge

6. temptation

7. aroma

8. luscious

9. pungent

10. savor

③ Build New Vocabulary

Context Clues

Read the passage below. Fill in each blank with the correct word from the shaded box.

edibleness	savored	devoured
lusciousness	blandness	tartness

The Bowl of Fruit

Timothy stared at the bowl of fruit on the table. He was unsure about

the _____ of the fruit it contained because when
he was younger he had eaten an apple from a bowl of fruit only to realize
that he was eating a piece of wax fruit. To be on the safe side, he picked

up a banana to make sure it was real. He _____ the
sweet smell of the ripe banana and knew that it was safe to eat.

There were four types of fruit in the bowl: bananas, oranges,
strawberries, and green grapes. Timothy decided to start with the

strawberries. He _____ the first strawberry and

was surprised by its _____, or total lack of flavor.

Timothy then decided to try some green grapes because they were

his favorite, and he was convinced of their _____.
So, he grabbed three grapes and popped them into his mouth. Soon the
smile on his face disappeared, and he puckered his lips. He could not get

over the _____ of the green grapes. Timothy
decided that he had eaten enough fruit for one day, and he learned a
valuable lesson: you cannot judge a fruit by its color!

4 Word Play

Word Puzzles

 Write the word from the Vocabulary List that best fits each clue. Then unscramble the circled letters to find the answer to the question below.

1. A heavenly smell

   ◯ __ __ __ __ __

2. Something you give in to

   ◯ __ ◯ __ __ __ ◯ __ __ __ __

3. What you do to a hard-fought victory

   __ __ __ __ ◯ __ __

4. Mashed potatoes without gravy

   __ __ __ ◯ __ __

5. What someone who is as hungry as a horse does to food

   __ __ __ __ __ ◯ __

6. Smells found in a fish market

   __ __ __ __ __ __ ◯ __

7. Fresh, ripe watermelon at a summer picnic

   __ __ __ __ __ __ __ ◯ __

What is a pastry that can talk?

A __ __ __ __ __ __ __ __ __ __

Government Vocabulary

1 **Word Meanings**

Word Choice

 Use the short definitions in the Vocabulary List to choose the vocabulary word in parentheses to complete each sentence. Circle the correct vocabulary word.

Vocabulary List

1. **diplomatic**
(dip´ lə mat´ ik) *adj.*
skilled with people

2. **decree**
(di krē´) *n.*
order or decision
made by a court

3. **monarchy**
(mon´ ər kē) *n.*
a nation ruled by a
king or queen

4. **constituent**
(kən stich´ ōō ənt) *n.*
voter

5. **tyrant**
(tī´ rənt) *n.*
cruel ruler

6. **truce**
(trōōs) *n.*
a temporary halt
to fighting

7. **veto**
(vē´ tō) *v.*
to reject a bill passed
by lawmaking body

8. **regulate**
(reg´ yə lāt´) *v.*
to manage or control
by rule

9. **bureau**
(byōōr´ ō) *n.*
government department
or office

10. **consensus**
(kən sen´ səs) *n.*
general agreement
or opinion

1. One job of the Federal Communications Commission is to *(regulate/ decree)* the kinds of things that are aired on television.

2. If the president does not agree with a bill passed by Congress, he can *(veto/monarchy)* it.

3. The Federal *(Bureau,/Consensus)* of Investigation is a government agency that investigates actions that threaten national security.

4. When the Japanese bombed Pearl Harbor, it was the *(consensus/delegation)* of Congress and the American people to declare war on Japan.

5. The early Roman emperor Caligula was a *(tyrant,/diplomatic)* who ruled by terror and oppression.

6. Before the American Revolution, the original thirteen colonies were ruled by the British *(bureau/monarchy)*.

7. The state senator was very concerned about her *(constituents/veto)*— the people who voted her into office.

8. A divorce *(decree/regulate)* is an example of a decision or order made by the court.

9. The two warring countries, weary and starving, decided to call a *(truce/tyrant)*.

10. An ambassador to a foreign country has to be *(diplomatic/truce)* when problems arise and try to solve problems peacefully.

2 Reference Skills

Synonyms

  The following are synonyms found in a thesaurus for words in this lesson's Vocabulary List. Find the synonyms in the dictionary. Choose the word from this lesson's Vocabulary List that best fits with the synonyms listed.

1. peace, armistice, cease-fire _____

2. manage, control, direct _____

3. reject, deny, dismiss _____

4. dictator, despot, ruler _____

5. committee, department, agency _____

6. agreement, consent, accord _____

• •

Use the synonyms above to complete the sentences below.

7. Charlemagne was a great _____ because he made many legal and economic changes that benefited his empire.

8. Before the invention of devices that allow people to see in the dark,

    a nighttime _____ was called during many battles to keep things fair.

9. It is not uncommon for a body to _____ an organ transplant.

10. A college consists of _____ that are in charge of teaching a specific subject.

11. When a car crash occurs, a police officer will

    _____ the traffic around the accident.

12. In 1867, William Seward made an _____ with Russia to purchase Alaska.

Vocabulary List

1. diplomatic

2. decree

3. monarchy

4. constituent

5. tyrant

6. truce

7. veto

8. regulate

9. bureau

10. consensus

③ Build New Vocabulary

Word Origins

Fill in the blanks with the word from the Vocabulary List that best fits.

1. _____ comes from the Latin word *diploma*, meaning "passport."

2. The Latin word *rex*, which means "king," is related to the word

_____, which means "to rule."

3. The literal meaning of the word _____ is "I forbid."

4. The word _____ comes from the Middle English word *trewes*, which means "agreements."

5. The word _____ comes from the Latin verb *decernere*, which means "to decide."

6. The word _____ is made up of a prefix that means "together" and the Latin word *sentire*, which means "to feel."

7. The word _____ is made from the prefix *mono-* and *archos*, which is the Latin word for "ruler."

8. The dinosaur *Tyrannosaurus Rex* shares the Greek root for the

word _____.

9. The word _____ comes from the French verb *constituer*, which means "to represent."

10. The word _____ is a French word that means "office."

● ●

🏅 Think About It

Remember that collegiate dictionaries contain the origins of most words with their definitions. If you are not sure about your answers above, try looking there.

Score _____ (Top Score 10)   Government Vocabulary • Build New Vocabulary

 **Word Play**

Poetry

 Fill in the blanks with the word from the Vocabulary List that rhymes or almost rhymes.

Change Is Good

The king said, "I do _____

that I am the leader of the land of Me!

Now go back to your own nation

so you can report the news to every TV station."

"But that is not fair," cried the man from the _____.

"You have no idea what I have to endure. Oh!

In my land of They, Them, and Us,

We never agree, we never reach _____!"

The king considered, "Well, I'm no _____.

In fact, I have even pardoned an ant!

Sometimes I just forget to be _____

and I do not mean to cause any static."

The man spoke quickly, "Then let's call a _____

and toast to our friendship using pineapple juice."

The king shook his head, "Sadly, I must _____

any food or drink that is not a burrito.

But that will not stop me from raising my glass

to my newfound friend who has so much class!

So here's to you and here's to me

Long live the improved _____."

Vocabulary for the Media

 1 **Word Meanings**

Analogies

Read each analogy below and figure out the relationship between each pair of words and/or phrases. Circle the vocabulary word that completes the analogy.

1. *(portray/retract)* is to *misrepresent* as *truth* is to *lie*

2. *(edit/verify)* is to *correct* as *fix* is to *repair*

3. *(slogan/agent)* is to *representative* as *reporter* is to *announcer*

4. *(slogan/reputation)* is to *motto* as *"Always Faithful"* is to *"All for one and one for all!"*

5. *(publish/edit)* is to *print* as *listen* is to *hear*

6. *(retract/edit)* is to *take back* as *deny* is to *reject*

7. *(reputation/tabloid)* is to *public opinion* as *happiness* is to *satisfaction*

8. *(monitor/tabloid)* is to *newspaper* as *journal* is to *magazine*

9. *(monitor/agent)* is to *watch* as *leave* is to *exit*

10. *(publish/verify)* is to *falsify* as *confirm* is to *lie*

Vocabulary List

1. **retract**
(ri trakt´) *v.*
to take back

2. **portray**
(por trā´) *v.*
to describe; to represent

3. **edit**
(ed´ it) *v.*
to prepare for publication or presentation

4. **tabloid**
(tab´ loid) *n.*
small newspaper

5. **monitor**
(mon´ i tər) *v.*
to check, watch, or listen to

6. **publish**
(pub´ lish) *v.*
to print

7. **reputation**
(rep´ yə tā´ shən) *n.*
general opinion of a person or thing

8. **agent**
(ā´ jənt) *n.*
person who acts for others

9. **slogan**
(slō´ gən) *n.*
a motto

10. **verify**
(ver´ ə fī´) *v.*
to confirm; to prove to be true

 Think About It

When trying to solve an analogy, remember these common relationships: synonyms, antonyms, examples.

Score _____ (Top Score 10)
Vocabulary for the Media • Word Meanings

2 Reference Skills

Multiple Meanings

 Read the dictionary entries for each word. Then fill in each blank with the correct word according to subject–verb agreement.

---

agent *n.* **1.** a person or organization that has the power to act for someone else: *The movie star's agent arranged the meeting.* **2.** something that produces or is able to produce a certain effect: *a cooling agent* **3.** an official in a government agency, especially a law-enforcement agency: *a CIA agent*

monitor *n.* **1.** a student with special duties in school, such as taking attendance: *the classroom monitor.* **2.** a device used to observe or record an activity or process: *a heart monitor* **3.** the part of a computer that has a screen that shows data: *We finally got a bigger monitor. v.* **1.** to check, watch, or listen to, as a radio or television transmission: *The president's advisors monitored the media for any new reports.* **2.** to supervise or watch over: *monitor someone's work*

---

1. When a natural disaster such as an earthquake occurs in a big city,

   insurance _____ become very busy.

2. In some cases, fire experts simply _____
   the progress of a forest fire to make sure that it does not get out
   of control.

3. In cases where arson is suspected, government

   _____ might be called in.

4. Different kinds of extinguishing _____ are
   used to put out different kinds of fires. For example, carbon dioxide,
   dry chemical, and foam are used for fires with flammable liquids.

5. An ambulance comes equipped with different

   _____ to assess a patient's health.

6. Police officers constantly _____ their radios
   for news of criminal activity.

Vocabulary List

1. retract
2. portray
3. edit
4. tabloid
5. monitor
6. publish
7. reputation
8. agent
9. slogan
10. verify

 3 Build New Vocabulary

Forming Nouns

Write the *noun* form of the vocabulary word in the blank. If you are unsure of spelling, refer to a dictionary.

1. retract + *-ion* = _____

2. edit + *-ion* = _____

3. verify + *-cation* = _____

4. Which word from the vocabulary list has the suffix *-ion?*

_____

 Write each word from above next to its definition.

5. the act of proving something to be true _____

6. the form in which a book or other written work is published

_____

7. general opinion of a person or thing _____

8. the act of taking back _____

 Fill in the blanks below with the correct word from above.

9. A bully on the playground has a bad _____.

10. When someone purchases a car, the dealer needs

_____ that he or she is a licensed driver.

11. If a newspaper prints false information, it needs to issue a

_____.

12. Book collectors get excited when they find a first

_____ of a rare book.

Word Play

What Am I Thinking Of?

Write the word from the Vocabulary List that answers each question below.

1. A cat does this with its claws, and a newspaper editor does this with a story that has the wrong information. What word am I thinking of?

   _____

2. Any good reporter should do this with the information she has written in an article before it is printed. What word am I thinking of?

   _____

3. This person can work for an insurance company, a sports star, or the government. What word am I thinking of? _____

4. If this were a member of a family, its big brother would be a newspaper such as *The Los Angeles Times,* and its little sister would be a weekly bulletin. What word am I thinking of?

   _____

5. "Keep your ear to the ground" is another way to say this. What word am I thinking of? _____

6. Fixing spelling errors is one way to do this. Whut werd ame eye thinkin uf? _____

7. "United we stand, divided we fall" is an example of this. What word am I thinking of? _____

8. You can do this to a book, newspaper, or magazine. What word am I thinking of? _____

9. This is something you can earn by doing something good or bad. What word am I thinking of? _____

10. An actor or actress does this. What word am I thinking of?

    _____

Vocabulary Review

1 **Review Word Meanings**

Read the passage below. Then answer the questions about the boldfaced vocabulary words.

Protecting Our Rain Forests

Rain forests are tropical woodlands and the **habitat** for a huge number of plant and animal species. In fact, as scientists have **verified,** rain forests contain more species of plants and animals than all of the rest of the world's ecosystems combined. Because rain forests contain such unique wildlife, they are closely **monitored** by ecologists.

Rain forests have existed for tens of millions of years, but **consumers** have caused the clearing of more than half. This is **detrimental** to the soil because when trees and plants are cut down and their roots no longer hold the soil in place, it becomes loose and sandy and is easily washed away by the rain.

It is the general **consensus** among environmentalists that, unless we stop **indulging** our urge to clear the forests away, our rain forests will be gone by early next century. They are pushing for more effective **regulation.** As our rain forests are **depleted,** so are the **robust** plants and animals that once lived there.

Now read the following questions. Then completely fill in the bubble of the correct answer.

1. What is the meaning of *robust,* based on the following analogy?
   robust is to *sickly*
   as *dark* is to *light*
   Ⓐ sickly
   Ⓑ dark
   Ⓒ healthy

2. What is the definition of *monitor* as it is used in the passage above?
   Ⓐ watch
   Ⓑ computer terminal
   Ⓒ control

3. Which sentence describes how clearing the rain forests is *detrimental* to the wildlife and/or plants?
   Ⓐ It kills species that are not found anywhere else in the world.
   Ⓑ It helps create new growth.
   Ⓒ It provides more shelter for animals.

4. Who wants more effective regulation for the rain forests?
   Ⓐ animals
   Ⓑ environmentalists
   Ⓒ politicians

5. If scientists *verify* something, then it is
   _____.
   Ⓐ incorrect
   Ⓑ ready
   Ⓒ true

6. According to the passage above, which is the definition of *deplete?*
   Ⓐ use up
   Ⓑ throw away
   Ⓒ fill up

7. In the passage above, what is the *habitat* that is discussed?
   Ⓐ the plant and animal species
   Ⓑ the rain forests
   Ⓒ erosion

8. What is a synonym for *consumer?*
   Ⓐ creator
   Ⓑ advertiser
   Ⓒ user

② Review Word Meanings

Read the passage below. Then answer the questions about the boldfaced vocabulary words.

Hunting Animals

Human beings have always been **predators**, hunting and killing other animals for food. American settlers hunted almost anything that was **edible**, especially when times were hard and people were dying from starvation. They chased deer and other animals from forests and shot **migrating** geese and other birds.

Settlers celebrated successful hunting by cooking a **luscious** meal, sending **aromas** of roast duck and venison floating throughout their homes. Some would give in to **temptation** and **devour** every bite, while others would eat slowly, **savoring** their food. Although most people do not have to hunt for food today, hunting is still an **intensely** popular sport. However, hunters receive a lot of criticism if they hunt animals for fun instead of for food.

⋯⋯⋯⋯⋯⋯⋯⋯⋯⋯⋯⋯⋯⋯⋯⋯⋯⋯⋯⋯⋯⋯⋯⋯⋯⋯⋯⋯⋯⋯⋯⋯

Now read the following questions. Then completely fill in the bubble of the correct answer.

1. Which of the following is closest in meaning to *devour?*
   - Ⓐ gobble
   - Ⓑ nibble
   - Ⓒ swallow

2. Which is a synonym for *savor?*
   - Ⓐ dislike
   - Ⓑ smell
   - Ⓒ enjoy

3. Which example sentence would be correct in a dictionary entry for *luscious* as it is used in the passage above?
   - Ⓐ The luscious earthquake left the city in ruins.
   - Ⓑ The dessert was absolutely luscious.
   - Ⓒ A luscious growth of plants circled their house.

4. Which of the following is closest in meaning to *aroma* as it is used in the passage above?
   - Ⓐ stink
   - Ⓑ sound
   - Ⓒ scent

5. Which word could replace *migrating* in the passage above?
   - Ⓐ moving
   - Ⓑ headache
   - Ⓒ arriving

6. Which of the following is an example of something that is *edible?*
   - Ⓐ forests
   - Ⓑ grocery stores
   - Ⓒ roast duck

7. In the passage above, what is labeled a *predator?*
   - Ⓐ human beings
   - Ⓑ deer
   - Ⓒ birds

8. Which is a synonym for *intense?*
   - Ⓐ fierce
   - Ⓑ gentle
   - Ⓒ warm

③ Review Word Meanings

Read the passage below. Then answer the questions about the boldfaced vocabulary words.

Where the Buffalo Roam

Early in our country's history, there were few laws that prevented the hunting of animals that were in danger of becoming extinct. An example is the buffalo that once roamed the North American plains in the millions and was in danger of dying out. Often, hunters would take only the buffalo's much-sought-after hide, leaving the body to **scavengers** or to waste.

Hunters such as Buffalo Bill Cody had a **reputation** for killing huge numbers of buffalo in a short amount of time, for sport and money. Cody's fame as a buffalo hunter landed him a role **portraying** himself in the plays of Ned Buntline, who **published** dime novels. Buffalo Bill was also a favorite subject of the **tabloids.**

Hunting buffalo seemed to be **contagious.** By 1895, when only 400 buffalo were left in the country, there was little hope for its **revival.** Finally, **constituents** began to demand that the government do something to protect American wildlife. One effective **agent** for change was Theodore Roosevelt, who pushed Congress to establish national parks as safe places for wildlife.

Now read the following questions. Then completely fill in the bubble of the correct answer.

1. Which of the following is an example of a *tabloid?*
   Ⓐ a pain reliever
   Ⓑ "Twinkle, Twinkle, Little Star"
   Ⓒ *The National Enquirer*

2. By 1895, there was little hope for the revival of what?
   Ⓐ dime novels
   Ⓑ buffalo
   Ⓒ Congress

3. Which of the following is the best example of something that is *published?*
   Ⓐ wildlife
   Ⓑ dime novels
   Ⓒ money

4. Which synonym could replace *contagious* in the passage above?
   Ⓐ catching
   Ⓑ friendly
   Ⓒ cautious

5. If the Latin word *reputare* means "to think over," then what does the word *reputation* mean?
   Ⓐ thorough research
   Ⓑ deep thoughtfulness
   Ⓒ overall quality or character

6. What is a synonym for *portray?*
   Ⓐ photograph
   Ⓑ represent
   Ⓒ read

7. What is another way of saying Theodore Roosevelt was an *agent* for change?
   Ⓐ Theodore Roosevelt acted as a representative for change.
   Ⓑ Theodore Roosevelt was hired by an environmentalist group to make changes.
   Ⓒ Theodore Roosevelt took part in undercover activities to make changes.

8. What is the definition of *constituent* as it is used in the passage above?
   Ⓐ person who elects government representatives
   Ⓑ hunter
   Ⓒ homeowner

Score _____ (Top Score 8)

Review Word Meanings

Read the passage below. Then answer the questions about the boldfaced vocabulary words.

Acid Rain

Acid rain is a serious, even **toxic**, threat to wildlife and plants all over the world, as well as to human beings. It is created, many **biologists** and other scientists believe, by the combination of nitrous oxides that come from industrial smokestacks with moisture from the atmosphere. These **pungent** clouds, containing nitric and sulfuric acid, can travel long distances before depositing their acids by rain. There is no way to **quarantine** a cloud. The once **bland**, nurturing rainwater now carries, and has carried since the Industrial Revolution, chemicals that poison everything it falls on.

The **symptoms** of acid rain are everywhere: the **erosion** of structures, the dying out of fish from rivers and streams, the destruction of forests. In some areas, acid rain is so bad that the trees look like they should be in an **infirmary**. Environmentalists send **delegations** to relate their concerns to local and national government bodies. There have been **decrees** that forced industries to strictly reduce the amount of harmful chemicals that are allowed to be emitted into the air.

Now read the following questions. Then completely fill in the bubble of the correct answer.

1. Which is the closest in meaning to *bland?*
   Ⓐ flavorful
   Ⓑ salty
   Ⓒ tasteless

2. Which word is not a synonym for *infirmary?*
   Ⓐ theater
   Ⓑ clinic
   Ⓒ hospital

3. Which of these items is *toxic* to wildlife?
   Ⓐ rainbows
   Ⓑ acid rain
   Ⓒ thunderstorms

4. What is the definition for *pungent?*
   Ⓐ a sharp taste or smell
   Ⓑ smell or taste with pleasure
   Ⓒ eat up greedily

5. According to the passage above, there is no way to *quarantine* _____.
   Ⓐ a bird
   Ⓑ acid rain
   Ⓒ a cloud

6. Which example sentence would be correct in a dictionary entry for *erosion?*
   Ⓐ I made an erosion in judgment.
   Ⓑ Erosion caused the house to fall into the ocean.
   Ⓒ Erosion is the study of water.

7. Which word is a synonym for *symptoms?*
   Ⓐ signs
   Ⓑ problems
   Ⓒ results

8. Which profession involves the study of plants and animals?
   Ⓐ athlete
   Ⓑ biologist
   Ⓒ dentist

9. Which word rhymes with *decree?*
   Ⓐ decorate
   Ⓑ dull
   Ⓒ flea

10. Environmentalists send _____ to relate their concerns to local and national government bodies?
    Ⓐ decrees
    Ⓑ depletion
    Ⓒ delegations

A Question of Value

1 **Word Meanings**

Shades of Meaning

Vocabulary List

1. **appraise**
   (ə prāz′) v.
   to judge the value of

2. **diminish**
   (di min′ ish) v.
   to make smaller

3. **insignificant**
   (in′ sig nif′ i kənt) adj.
   unimportant

4. **investment**
   (in vest′ mənt) n.
   use of money to
   make money

5. **premium**
   (prē′ mē əm) n.
   a high or unusual value

6. **indispensable**
   (in′ di spen′ sə bəl) adj.
   absolutely necessary

7. **inferior**
   (in fir′ ē ər) adj.
   of poor quality

8. **superior**
   (sə pir′ ē ər) adj.
   more or better

9. **superfluous**
   (soō pûr′ floo əs) adj.
   more than is needed

10. **barter**
    (bär′ tər) v.
    to trade

 Choose the word from the Vocabulary List that best matches each set of synonyms listed below. Look up the synonyms in the dictionary if necessary.

1. evaluate, judge, value _____

2. small, unimportant, meaningless _____

3. essential, necessary, vital _____

4. decrease, decline, lessen _____

5. superior, prime, excellent _____

6. trade, haggle, exchange _____

7. unnecessary, excessive, needless _____

8. premium, superb, preferred _____

9. second-rate, mediocre, substandard _____

10. venture, risk, stocks _____

 Think About It

If you cannot figure out which word from the Vocabulary List matches each set of synonyms, create a sentence that works for all three synonyms in each set. Then place the vocabulary word you think matches the set in the sentence. If the meaning of the sentence is similar to the others, then you have found the correct synonym.

Reference Skills

Multiple Meanings

Read the dictionary entry for *barter* below. Then answer the questions that follow.

> **barter** *v.t.* to trade (goods) for other goods: *barter sugar for clothing.* *v.i.* to trade by bartering goods: *The merchants bartered in the marketplace.* *n.* **1.** the act or practice of bartering: *Barter is a popular activity among these people.* **2.** something bartered

1. What does *v.t.* stand for? _____ What does this

   mean? _____

2. What does *v.i.* stand for? _____ What does this

   mean? _____

3. Name a reference book other than a dictionary that would explain the difference between a direct and an indirect object.

   _____

• •

Write the correct definition of *barter* for each sentence below based on the context. If *barter* is used as a verb, write whether the verb is transitive or intransitive.

4. Native Americans often *bartered* to get food and goods that they

   could not make or grow themselves. _____

   _____

5. Early trappers used beaver pelts as *barter.* _____

   _____

6. Children often *barter* their own toys for their friends' toys.

   _____

   _____

Vocabulary List

1. *appraise*

2. *diminish*

3. *insignificant*

4. *investment*

5. *premium*

6. *indispensable*

7. *inferior*

8. *superior*

9. *superfluous*

10. *barter*

③ Build New Vocabulary

Word Parts

 Below are some of the word parts used in this lesson's Vocabulary List, along with their meanings and related word parts. Use these parts to make new words, as shown. Look up each new word in the dictionary to check the spelling and the definition.

> **insignificant:** *in-* (not); *signifare* (to indicate; to mean; from *signum*, which means "sign")

1. *re-* (back; backward) + *signare* (to sign, to seal) =

   _____: to quit

2. *con-* (with; together; thoroughly) + *signum* =

   _____: to give over to another's care

> **superfluous:** *super-* (over; higher; surpassing others of its kind) + *fluere* (to flow)

3. *super-* + *intendere* (to stretch out) = _____:
   someone who directs the work of something

4. *super-* + *videre* (to see) = _____: to oversee

• •

 Fill in the blanks with the correct form of a word you formed above that best fits the context of each sentence below.

5. President Nixon _____ as president in 1974 as a result of his participation in the Watergate scandal.

6. As commander in chief of the armed forces, the president

   _____ the leaders of the armed forces.

7. The _____ met with the school board to discuss the future of the city's schools.

8. The workers in the supplies department _____ uniforms and weapons to the new recruits.

Word Play

Connotation

Read each pair of words below. Fill in the blank with the word that has a more positive connotation. If both words have similar connotation, write *neutral* in the blank.

1. barter   haggle   _____

2. appraise   guess   _____

3. diminish   reduce   _____

4. insignificant minor   _____

5. investment   stake   _____

6. premium   bonus   _____

7. indispensable vital   _____

8. inferior   secondary   _____

9. superior   better   _____

10. superfluous extra   _____

Vocabulary about Amounts

1 **Word Meanings**

Complete the Passage

Read the following passage and fill in the blanks with the appropriate word from the Vocabulary List. Read it again slowly to make certain the story makes sense.

A Great Idea

During World War II, the government created the Office of Price

Administration to determine _____ of goods that were valuable to the war effort. This way the government could ensure that materials needed for the war would not be wasted by

civilians. Before the war, there was an _____ supply of goods such as automobile tires and gasoline. During the war, however, supplies such as these were needed for military

equipment. The _____ of, or most, Americans accepted rationing as part of war; however, a small

_____ bought rationed items illegally.

One technique used to ration was the distribution of ration books

that held coupons. If you wanted to _____ more coupons, you had to fill out several forms; many people grew "victory gardens" to add to their food supply instead. Even people in

areas where fertile land was _____ tried their hand at growing their own produce.

The cost of the war to all countries involved was

_____ at $1 trillion—the

_____ to a million millions! After the war, most

salespeople found it easy to fill their _____—or the amount of items they were required to sell. The war had helped get the country out of the Great Depression. More families were able to spend money on goods and entertainment. A family might enjoy a

night out listening to the music of a _____, or a group of five musicians. After the Depression and the war, the 1950s certainly were "Happy Days" for many people.

Vocabulary List

1. **accumulate**
   (ə kū′ myə lāt′) v.
   to collect

2. **ample**
   (am′ pəl) adj.
   more than enough

3. **quota**
   (kwō′ tə) n.
   required amount or part

4. **ration**
   (rash′ ən) n.
   a definite or fixed amount

5. **tabulate**
   (tab′ yə lāt′) v.
   to add up

6. **equivalent**
   (i kwiv′ ə lənt) adj.
   equal in value

7. **majority**
   (mə jôr′ i tē) n.
   larger part

8. **minority**
   (mə nor′ i tē) n.
   smaller part

9. **quintet**
   (kwin tet′) n.
   group of five

10. **sparse**
    (spärs) adj.
    thinly spread or scattered

② Reference Skills

Multiple Meanings

 Read each dictionary entry below. Fill in the blanks with the correct word and write the number of the definition you used in the box.

---

minority *n.* **1.** the smaller part of a group or whole: *A minority of voters opposed the levy.* **2.** a group that is different from the rest of the general population, such as in religion, race, or politics: *Native Americans are an example of a minority in the United States and Canada.* **3.** a group or political party having fewer than half of the members of the whole: *Some years, the Democrats are the minority in Congress.*

ration *n.* **1.** a fixed portion: *The woman received her ration of beef.* **2.** amount of food allowed daily, such as for a soldier.; *v.* **1.** to give out in portions **2.** to limit to fixed portions.

quintet *n.* **1.** a musical composition made for five voices or five musical instruments **2.** a musical group made up of five performers **3.** any group of five

---

1. The Jackson Five was a popular —————————— in the 1970s. ☐

2. In some countries, people are allowed only a —————————— of a product that is hard to come by. ☐

3. The ———————— party often struggles to get the bills it wants enacted. ☐

4. Most students accepted the school's new dress code; only a small —————————— protested. ☐

5. The five friends at Quincy Middle School were together so often that they were called the Quincy ————————. ☐

6. During the Cold War, the Soviet government —————————— people's food supplies. ☐

Vocabulary List

1. accumulate
2. ample
3. quota
4. ration
5. tabulate
6. equivalent
7. majority
8. minority
9. quintet
10. sparse

3 Build New Vocabulary

Related Words

Many of the words in the Vocabulary List have other words related to them. Match each word below to its definition by writing the letter of the definition in the box. Then write the related vocabulary word in the blank.

1. ☐ rationale _____

2. ☐ equivocal _____

3. ☐ amplifier _____

4. ☐ quintuple _____

5. ☐ quotient _____

6. ☐ majorette _____

7. ☐ cumulative _____

a. a device for increasing the strength of an electronic signal

b. a number obtained by dividing one number by another number

c. made up of collected parts

d. having more than one possible meaning

e. a baton twirler who accompanies a marching band

f. a reasonable or logical basis

g. five times as great or as many

Score _____ (Top Score 14)   Vocabulary about Amounts • Build New Vocabulary

 **Word Play**

Riddles and Clues

 Write the word from the Vocabulary List that answers each clue below.

1. what rules in the U.S. Congress _____

2. what one hundred pennies and one dollar are

   _____

3. to collect many cars, dolls, or coins _____

4. during World War II, the government did this to things like meat,

   automobile tires, coffee, sugar, and gas _____

5. The Jackson Five and The Dionne Quintuplets

   _____

6. not meager _____

7. what salespeople fill _____

8. to add numbers in columns _____

9. like hair on a balding man's head _____

10. opposite of majority _____

• •

Think About It

If you are having a hard time solving a riddle or clue, try looking up unfamiliar words in a dictionary or using an encyclopedia or the Internet to find out more about unfamiliar people or places.

Number Prefixes

1 **Word Meanings**

Word Choice

1. **trimester**
   (trī´ mes tər) *n.*
   period of three months

2. **trilogy**
   (tril´ ə jē) *n.*
   series of three closely
   related works

3. **monopoly**
   (mə nop´ ə lē) *n.*
   total control of
   something

4. **monorail**
   (mon´ ə rāl´) *n.*
   single-rail railway
   system

5. **monocle**
   (mon´ ə kəl) *n.*
   eyeglass for one eye

6. **biped**
   (bī´ ped) *n.*
   two-footed animal

7. **bisect**
   (bī´ sekt) *v.*
   to divide into two
   equal parts

8. **bilingual**
   (bī ling´ gwəl) *adj.*
   able to speak two
   languages

9. **centennial**
   (sen ten´ ē əl) *n.*
   a hundredth
   anniversary

10. **millennium**
    (mi len´ ē əm) *n.*
    period of a
    thousand years

 Read each sentence below. Use the context clues to choose the word in parentheses that best completes each sentence. Circle your answer.

1. President Theodore Roosevelt is often pictured wearing a *(monorail/monocle)*, which he used to correct vision in one eye.

2. The *(biped/bilingual)* dinosaurs, called *pachycephalosaurs,* walked on two feet.

3. A *(monorail/trimester)*—made up of vehicles guided by one rail or beam instead of two—is a popular form of transportation in many large cities.

4. Because it has no other competitors, the U.S. Postal Service has a *(monocle/monopoly)* on the business of delivering letters.

5. A *(bisected/trilogy)* circle is made of two semicircles.

6. The need to become *(bilingual/biped)*, especially in Spanish or Japanese, is growing rapidly in the United States.

7. J.R.R. Tolkein wrote a popular *(trilogy, monopoly)* made up of the books *The Fellowship of the Ring, The Two Towers,* and *The Return of the King.*

8. The United States celebrated its *(centennial/millennium)* in 1876.

9. A pregnancy is divided into three *(trimesters/bisects)*, or three-month periods.

10. The new *(millennium/centennial)* actually began in the year 2001; the last thousand-year period began in 1001 and ended in 2000.

2 Reference Skills

Dictionary Skills

 Below are some common number prefixes. Look up each prefix in the dictionary and write its definition in the blank. Then write the words from this lesson's Vocabulary List next to the prefix they begin with.

1. *mono-* _____

_____

2. *bi-* _____

_____

3. *mill-* _____

_____

4. *tri-* _____

_____

5. *cent-* _____

_____

• •

Look up the following number prefixes in the dictionary and write their definitions in the blanks. Use the words given below as clues to the meaning of each prefix.

6. *quadr-* _____ quadrant

7. *deca-* _____ decathlon

8. *semi-* _____ semicircle

9. *uni-* _____ unicycle

10. *multi-* _____ multicolored

11. *penta-* _____ pentagon

12. *oct-* _____ octopus

Vocabulary List

1. trimester
2. trilogy
3. monopoly
4. monorail
5. monocle
6. biped
7. bisect
8. bilingual
9. centennial
10. millennium

3 Build New Vocabulary

Word Parts

Below are some of the word parts found in this lesson's Vocabulary List, along with their meanings. Use these word parts to make new words, as shown. Use the dictionary for help.

> **trimester:** *tri-* (three) + *-mester* (from *mensis,* which means "month") = three months

1. *sex-* (six) + *-mester* = _____

2. *tri-* + *-pod* (feet) = _____

> **bisect:** *bi-* (two) + *-sect* (to cut) = to cut in two

3. *inter-* (between; among) + *-sect* = _____

4. *bi-* + *lateral* (side) = _____

> **monopoly:** *mono-* (one) + *poly* (many) = one that controls many

5. *poly-* + *glotta* (language) = _____

6. *mono-* + *tonos* (tone) = _____

> **millennium:** *mill-* (thousand) + *-ennium* (year) = a thousand years

7. *mill-* + *ped* (foot) = _____

8. *per-* (throughout) + *ennial* _____

• •

Think About It

Did you check to see if the new words you created really exist in the dictionary? Sometimes there are spelling changes when two word parts are added together to make a new word.

Score _____ (Top Score 8)   Number Prefixes • Build New Vocabulary

 **Word Play**

Silly Clues

 Write the word from the Vocabulary List that is related to each silly clue listed below.

1. It might take a millipede this long to walk a thousand miles.

   _____

2. This is what it is called when one party, or person, has exclusive

   ownership of a commodity. _____

3. This can apply to a pregnancy or college courses.

   _____

4. The town had waited a hundred years to celebrate this.

   _____

5. *Green Eggs and Ham; Pink Rice and Spam; Brown Toast and Jam.*

   These three books might be a _____ written
   by Dr. Seuss.

6. The teacher is able to speak English and Klingon!

   _____

7. Put two of these together, and you have one pair of eyeglasses.

   _____

8. One way to dissect a frog. _____

9. This is a train minus one rail. _____

10. They walk upright. _____

Vocabulary List

1. **compatible**
   (kəm pat′ ə bəl) *adj.*
   able to exist together

2. **fraternal**
   (frə tûr′ nəl) *adj.*
   brotherly

3. **welfare**
   (wel′ fâr) *n.*
   well-being

4. **acquaintance**
   (ə kwān′ təns) *n.*
   person you know

5. **reconcile**
   (rek′ ən sīl) *v.*
   to bring into harmony
   or friendship

6. **interdependent**
   (in′ tər di pen′ dənt)
   adj. depending on
   each other

7. **discretion**
   (di skresh′ ən) *n.*
   good judgment; caution

8. **client**
   (klī′ ənt) *n.*
   customer of a business

9. **chaperon**
   (shap′ ə rōn′) *n.*
   person who watches
   young people

10. **mentor**
    (men′ tər) *n.*
    trusted advisor

Relationships

1 **Word Meanings**

Which Word?

 Use the clues below to figure out which vocabulary word best completes each sentence. Write the word in the blank.

1. One of the goals of the Constitution is to "promote the general

   _____" of the people of the United States.
   (Clue: well-being)

2. The states were _____ because they relied on
   each other for trade as well as military protection. **(Clue: dependent)**

3. The Constitutional Convention met in 1787 to create a constitution

   that would be _____ with most of the needs of
   the states of the union. **(Clue: agreeable)**

4. Many of the men who attended the Constitutional Convention were

   friends, or at least _____. **(Clue: people)**

5. Some delegates knew each other so well that their relationship was

   almost _____. **(Clue: brotherly)**

6. Some of their sessions were stormy, but the delegates often tried to

   _____ after any angry outburst. **(Clue: harmony)**

7. The delegates did not take their job lightly—they used a lot of

   _____ and care in the construction of the
   Constitution. **(Clue: judgment)**

8. Of course, the delegates did not need a _____,
   because they were all grown men who could take care of themselves.
   (Clue: watches)

9. American citizens could be called the _____ of
   the Constitutional Convention, because the Constitution was created
   on their behalf. **(Clue: customers)**

10. The delegates at the Constitutional Convention became

    _____ to many politicians who followed
    them. **(Clue: advisor)**

2 Reference Skills

Multiple Meanings

 Read the dictionary entries below. Then fill in each blank with the correct form of the word that completes the sentence. Finally, write the number of the definition you used in the box.

acquaintance *n.* **1.** a person you know but are not good friends with: *The doctors were acquaintances.* **2.** relationship between people who are not close friends: *I had an acquaintance with her when I was in college.* **3.** knowledge of something; familiarity: *Because my mother is a veterinarian, I have a strong acquaintance of animals.*

reconcile *v.* **1.** to make friendly again, as after a fight: *After fighting over a toy, the brothers reconciled.* **2.** to cause (someone) to accept something unpleasant: *She reconciled herself to her life of poverty.* **3.** to make consistent with; to make agree: *The mother tried to reconcile the two different versions of the stories.*

1. Many members of the Continental Congress who signed the Declaration of Independence, having met before, were _____. ☐

2. The colonists refused to _____ themselves to a life ruled by Great Britain. ☐

3. It took a long time after the Revolutionary War for the United States and Great Britain to _____. ☐

4. A lawyer and member of the Virginia House of Burgesses, Patrick Henry had a strong _____ of law and politics. ☐

5. The lawyer had to _____ the three different accounts of the burglary before he could put the witnesses on the stand. ☐

6. Thomas Jefferson studied law under a man named George Wythe, who was much more than an _____—Jefferson called him his "second father." ☐

Vocabulary List

1. compatible

2. fraternal

3. welfare

4. acquaintance

5. reconcile

6. interdependent

7. discretion

8. client

9. chaperon

10. mentor

3 Build New Vocabulary

The Prefix *dis-*

Write each word from the box below next to its correct definition. Use a dictionary if you need help.

discharge	discontinue	discourage
discredit	disgraceful	discord
disillusion	disloyal	disobedient
displeasure		

1. to destroy belief in _____

2. to release _____

3. the state of being annoyed _____

4. refusing to carry out orders _____

5. not faithful _____

6. lack of agreement or harmony _____

7. to free from a false idea _____

8. shameful _____

9. to lessen the hope or confidence of _____

10. to stop _____

• •

Write the Vocabulary List word that best completes each sentence below.

11. A _____ should never be disloyal because his or her job is to provide good advice to people who need guidance.

12. At first two people may seem _____, but when they get to know each other, they may experience nothing but discord.

 **Word Play**

Idioms and Similes

 Each clue below has an idiom or simile in it. Write the letter of the vocabulary word that matches each clue.

1. This means *"as close as brothers."* _____

2. This person should be *as watchful as a hawk.* _____

3. Someone who uses this does not *throw caution to the wind.* _____

4. The opposite of *"at odds with"* _____

5. People who are like *two peas in a pod* are this. _____

6. This person could be called a *guiding light.* _____

7. *"You can't have one without the other."* _____

a. discretion

b. fraternal

c. interdependent

d. compatible

e. mentor

f. reconciled

g. chaperon

• •

 Now use one of the idioms or similes from above to complete each sentence below.

8. People who like to skydive

_____.

9. A new mother is _____.

10. During the Civil War, the North was

_____ the South.

11. Best friends are like _____.

12. A _____ will help you make a difficult decision.

Vocabulary List

1. **benevolence**
   (bə nev´ ə ləns) *n.*
   kindness; good will

2. **benign**
   (bi nīn´) *adj.*
   gentle; not harmful

3. **benediction**
   (ben´ i dik´ shən) *n.*
   a blessing

4. **cosmologist**
   (koz mä´ lə jist) *n.*
   person who studies the
   universe

5. **cosmos**
   (koz´ mōs) *n.*
   the orderly universe

6. **sympathize**
   (sim´ pə thīz´) *v.*
   to share in another's
   emotions

7. **pathetic**
   (pə thet´ ik) *adj.*
   arousing pity
   or sadness

8. **fortitude**
   (for´ tə tood´) *n.*
   courage or strength
   to endure

9. **forte**
   (fôrt) *n.*
   a person's strong point

10. **fortify**
    (for´ tə fī´) *v.*
    to make strong

Latin and Greek Roots

 Word Meanings

Analogies

 Write the word from the Vocabulary List that completes each analogy below.

1. _____ is to *evil*
   as *nice* is to *mean*

2. _____ is to *universe*
   as *astronomer* is to *space*

3. _____ is to *weaken*
   as *live* is to *die*

4. _____ is to *happy*
   as *giant* is to *dwarf*

5. _____ is to *blessing*
   as *house* is to *dwelling*

6. _____ is to *strong point*
   as *absent* is to *missing*

7. _____ is to *harshness*
   as *happiness* is to *depression*

8. _____ is to *universe*
   as *moon* is to *satellite*

9. _____ is to a *survivor*
   as *cowardice* is to a *deserter*

10. _____ is to *make fun of*
    as *strength* is to *weakness*

② Reference Skills

Word Choice

 Read the thesaurus and shortened dictionary entries below. Study the definitions and example phrases for each word. Then complete the following sentences by writing the word that best fits.

> **Thesaurus**
>
>   **benign** *adj.* harmless; gracious
>
> **Dictionary**
>
>   **harmless** *adj.* not having the ability to cause harm: *harmless spider*
>
>   **gracious** *adj.* having or showing courtesy, kindness, and tact: *a gracious host*

1. When the unhappy diner complained about the food, the

_____ owner offered his apologies, a free

meal, and a gift certificate.

2. Chicken pox is irritating but most often _____

to children.

> **Thesaurus**
>
>   **fortify** *v.* reinforce; armor; arm
>
> **Dictionary**
>
>   **reinforce** *v.* to fortify or make more effective; strengthen
>
>   **armor** *v.* to outfit or cover with metal
>
>   **arm** *v.* to provide with weapons

3. Children complete homework assignments to

_____ the skills their teachers have taught them.

4. An effective military _____ its troops with the
latest advances in technology.

5. During the Middle Ages, squires had to _____
knights so that they would be protected against arrows and swords.

Vocabulary List

1. benevolence

2. benign

3. benediction

4. cosmologist

5. cosmos

6. sympathize

7. pathetic

8. fortitude

9. forte

10. fortify

3 Build New Vocabulary

Context Clues

 Read each root word below and circle its meaning.

1. *bene-*   good   bad

2. *cosm-*   cause   universe

3. *fort-*   feel   strong

• •

 Read the sentences below. Choose the word from the box that best completes each sentence and write it in the blank.

fortification	beneficial	benefactor
cosmopolitan	fortress	

4. A person who travels the world and speaks many different languages

   is _____.

5. Sandbags are often used for _____ during a flood.

6. Sunlight is _____ to the growth of most plants and flowers.

7. The Tower of London, the home of the Crown Jewels, is an example

   of a _____.

8. Andrew Carnegie liked to help others, so he became a

   _____ to many libraries throughout the world.

4 Word Play

Rhymes and Examples

 Read the rhymes below. Fill in the blank with the vocabulary word that best completes each rhyme.

1. Basketball was not his _____, but he loved to play croquet.

2. Before they ate dinner—and this is not fiction—the family paused and said a _____.

3. In all of the places in all of the _____, he liked to live in the place called Oz most.

4. "Come," said the nurse, "and stand in this line, but only if your disease is _____."

5. "I _____," said the actor to the detective, "with your need to wear a disguise."

 Read the examples below. Then choose the vocabulary word that best matches each example and write the letter of the word you chose in the blank.

6. _____ a puppy with sad eyes

7. _____ helping an elderly woman cross the street

8. _____ a professional stargazer

9. _____ to prepare a castle for invasion

10. _____ the Little Engine That Could

a. fortify

b. cosmologist

c. benevolence

d. fortitude

e. pathetic

Vocabulary Review

1 **Review Word Meanings**

Read the passage below. Then answer the questions about the boldfaced
vocabulary words.

Mother Teresa

Widely thought of as one of the most **benevolent** people of the previous
millennium, Mother Teresa was a nun who devoted her life to caring for the
poor and sick. She served as the principal of a Catholic high school in Calcutta,
India, where disease and poverty were everywhere. Moved by the sick and dying
homeless people in the streets around her, Mother Teresa sought to **diminish**
their suffering.

In 1948, she was given permission to leave her post and devote herself to her
clients—the needy of Calcutta. She soon became **indispensable** to her new
ministry. From helping to provide health care and food supplies to saying a
benediction for the poor, Mother Teresa worked tirelessly for decades. For her
efforts in providing comfort where it once was **sparse** and in **fortifying** the poor
and sick, she was awarded the Nobel Peace Prize in 1979.

Now read the following questions. Then completely
fill in the bubble of the correct answer.

1. What is the meaning of *benevolence* based
   on the following analogy?
   Benevolence is to *meanness*
   as *happiness* is to *sadness*
   Ⓐ meanness
   Ⓑ kindness
   Ⓒ happiness

2. Which of the following is a synonym for
   indispensable?
   Ⓐ stubborn
   Ⓑ needed
   Ⓒ unimportant

3. _____ were Mother Teresa's clients.
   Ⓐ The needy of Calcutta
   Ⓑ The nuns of Calcutta
   Ⓒ The happy of Calcutta

4. Mother Teresa would _____ a benediction
   for the poor.
   Ⓐ eat
   Ⓑ say
   Ⓒ grow

5. Which of the following could replace *sparse*
   in the passage?
   Ⓐ scattered
   Ⓑ thick
   Ⓒ fight

6. What is the definition of *fortify?*
   Ⓐ get older
   Ⓑ construct a building
   Ⓒ strengthen

7. Mother Teresa sought to diminish the
   suffering of _____.
   Ⓐ principals
   Ⓑ homeless people
   Ⓒ nuns

8. What is the definition of *millennium?*
   Ⓐ a thousand years
   Ⓑ a many-legged insect
   Ⓒ a reference book

Score _____ (Top Score 8)

② Review Word Meanings

Read the passage below. Then answer the questions about the boldfaced vocabulary words.

Andrew Carnegie

Andrew Carnegie was an American industrialist who built a fortune and, with care and **discretion,** gave a great deal of it to charity. At the age of 14, **chaperoned** by his parents, he left his native Scotland and came to Pennsylvania in the United States.

A **superior** worker, Carnegie quickly moved from good jobs to better jobs. He first worked in a cotton mill for $1.20 a week, tirelessly filling his **quota.** The next year he learned how to use the telegraph and soon found himself working for the Pennsylvania Railroad, which **bisected** much of the country. He made smart **investments** in oil lands and in companies such as the Pullman Company. Before he knew it, he was wealthy.

Carnegie used his **ample** money supply to build an empire in the iron and steel industry. He thought that so much money for one family was **superfluous** and set out to donate it to causes that he thought would serve not just a **minority** of people, but the population as a whole as well. In his lifetime, he **rationed** out more than $350 million to various educational, cultural, and peace institutions.

Now read the following questions. Then completely fill in the bubble of the correct answer.

1. Which of the following is a definition of *ample?*
   Ⓐ more than enough
   Ⓑ an amount that is less than what is used
   Ⓒ an equal amount

2. Carnegie was known as a _____ worker.
   Ⓐ superfluous
   Ⓑ ample
   Ⓒ superior

3. What is the meaning of *minority* as it is used in the passage?
   Ⓐ the state of being under legal age
   Ⓑ a group or political party having fewer than half of the votes
   Ⓒ the smaller part of a group

4. What does *bisected* mean in the passage?
   Ⓐ divided the country into two parts
   Ⓑ divided the country into three parts
   Ⓒ divided the country unevenly

5. Which word could replace *superfluous* in the passage?
   Ⓐ too little
   Ⓑ excessive
   Ⓒ superior

6. Carnegie made investments in _____.
   Ⓐ oil lands
   Ⓑ Scotland
   Ⓒ cotton mills

7. Which dictionary definition below describes how *ration* is used in the passage?
   Ⓐ a fixed portion
   Ⓑ to give out in portions
   Ⓒ to use sparingly

8. Who chaperoned Carnegie to the United States?
   Ⓐ his company
   Ⓑ his parents
   Ⓒ his empire

③ Review Word Meanings

Read the passage below. Then answer the questions about the boldfaced vocabulary words.

Harriet Tubman

Born a slave in 1820, Harriet Tubman had the **fortitude** to save herself and hundreds of others from slavery. The **majority** of people would agree that she had a gift for helping others. She worked as a field hand and house servant on a Maryland plantation, and, in 1849, she could no longer take the life of slavery that had been imposed on her since birth. Tired of being treated as an **inferior** human being who was as **insignificant** as a piece of furniture and could be **bartered** away from her family at a moment's notice, she escaped her life of slavery and fled to the North.

Because she **sympathized** with her fellow slaves, Tubman made 19 trips back and forth from the South to the North and Canada to help others reach freedom. Each time she risked her own freedom and even her life. Southern states paid a **premium** to those who captured fleeing slaves. In all, Tubman helped more than 300 slaves—strangers, **acquaintances,** and her own family—to freedom on the Underground Railroad.

. . . .

Now read the following questions. Then completely fill in the bubble of the correct answer.

1. Which of the following would most likely be an *acquaintance* of Harriet Tubman?
   Ⓐ her best friend
   Ⓑ her mother
   Ⓒ person on another plantation

2. What is the definition of *insignificant* as it is used in the passage?
   Ⓐ huge
   Ⓑ unimportant
   Ⓒ unclear

3. What does the Latin root *fort-* in *fortitude* mean?
   Ⓐ weakness
   Ⓑ calm
   Ⓒ strength

4. What does *premium* mean in the passage?
   Ⓐ of high quality
   Ⓑ something given at a reduced price
   Ⓒ a reward or payment for something

5. How are *equivalent* and *unequal* related?
   Ⓐ They are synonyms.
   Ⓑ They are antonyms.
   Ⓒ They are both nouns.

6. What does *majority* mean in the passage?
   Ⓐ equal parts
   Ⓑ less than half
   Ⓒ more than half

7. Which of the following is an antonym for *inferior?*
   Ⓐ second-rate
   Ⓑ excellent
   Ⓒ used

8. Who did Harriet Tubman sympathize with?
   Ⓐ Canadians
   Ⓑ other slaves
   Ⓒ strangers

4 Review Word Meanings

Read the passage below. Then answer the questions about the boldfaced vocabulary words.

Florence Nightingale

Florence Nightingale's **forte** was tending to the sick and dying. But this British woman, born in 1820, was much more than a **benign** nurse. After pursuing a classical education, she decided that the field of study she felt most **compatible** with was nursing. She studied nursing for almost a **quintet** of years and was put in charge of a London hospital for bedridden women.

After the Crimean War in eastern Europe broke out in 1854, Nightingale was concerned about the **welfare** of the sick and wounded soldiers. She requested to go and help, and the British war minister, **appraising** the situation, assigned her to lead all nursing operations at the war front.

By the time the warring sides had **reconciled,** Nightingale and her team of nurses had reduced the death rate at the hospital from 42 percent to 2 percent. She is considered to be the founder of modern nursing because she recognized that nurses and doctors were **interdependent** and that doctors should not have a **monopoly** on higher-level patient care. Nightingale founded the first professional nursing school and wrote three books—though they are not a **trilogy**—on nursing as a medical profession.

Now read the following questions. Then completely fill in the bubble of the correct answer.

1. Which of the following is an antonym for *benign?*
   - Ⓐ serious
   - Ⓑ unkind
   - Ⓒ tasteless

2. If a person's *forte* is tending to the sick, then a good job for him or her would be which of the following?
   - Ⓐ English teacher
   - Ⓑ construction worker
   - Ⓒ nurse

3. What is the definition of *reconciled* as it is used in the passage?
   - Ⓐ tore apart
   - Ⓑ made up
   - Ⓒ considered

4. How many books are in a *trilogy?*
   - Ⓐ three
   - Ⓑ four
   - Ⓒ two

5. Which of the following is a synonym for *compatible?*
   - Ⓐ agreeing
   - Ⓑ unfriendly
   - Ⓒ patriotic

6. Which of the following is an example of a *quintet?*
   - Ⓐ twins
   - Ⓑ a classroom of ten students
   - Ⓒ a musical group with five members

7. Which of the following could be substituted for *welfare* in the passage?
   - Ⓐ money
   - Ⓑ well-being
   - Ⓒ fee

8. Nurses and _____ are interdependent.
   - Ⓐ mothers
   - Ⓑ doctors
   - Ⓒ war ministers

Cumulative Review

Definitions

 Write the vocabulary word that matches each definition below.
(**Hint:** The words may appear in any lesson throughout the book.)

1. equal in value *adj.* _____

2. good judgment; caution *n.* _____

3. sameness of pitch *adj.* _____

4. small newspaper *n.* _____

5. leaves on a tree or plant *n.* _____

6. a pleasant odor *n.* _____

7. remain suspended in the air; linger *v.* _____

8. trade *v.* _____

9. in time order *adj.* _____

10. bring back to consciousness *v.* _____

11. overused saying *n.* _____

12. false charge *n.* _____

13. showing off *adj.* _____

14. dart about *v.* _____

15. boldness *n.* _____

Score _____ (Top Score 15)

Synonyms

 Choose the vocabulary word from the box that is a synonym for each word below. Write the vocabulary word in the blank. (**Hint:** Each word is used once.)

inverted	skeptical	jovial	punctual	immortal
ingenious	compulsory	flail	undergo	blurt
filthy	contagious	superfluous	fraternal	constituent

1. exclaim _____

2. excess _____

3. merry _____

4. everlasting _____

5. doubtful _____

6. experience _____

7. reversed _____

8. member _____

9. thrash _____

10. transmittable _____

11. clever _____

12. timely _____

13. brotherly _____

14. required _____

15. dirty _____

Sentence Completion

Write the vocabulary word that best completes each sentence below. Each sentence contains a clue related to a lesson theme. (**Hint:** The words may appear in any lesson throughout the book.)

1. It is a good idea to make _____ plans with a friend if you do not know what time you will complete your homework.

2. At a French restaurant a _____ might order a cream puff for dessert.

3. A lawyer will _____ a jury's decision if he or she feels an injustice has occurred during a trial.

4. People will call you _____ if you believe that walking under a ladder will bring you bad luck.

5. If the media announces an incorrect piece of information, it has to

_____ what was said.

6. In the human life cycle it is _____ to eat properly and stay in shape.

7. During an election, the board of elections has to

_____ the number of votes each candidate receives.

8. When reporting the news, journalists have to be

_____ so they do not choose one side of the story over another.

9. During the 1930s, the Italian government was controlled by a

_____ named Benito Mussolini.

10. It is not a good idea to make a quick movement if you want to

_____ along a beach and enjoy the sunset.

Score _____ (Top Score 10)

Words and Themes

 Choose two words from the box that belong with each theme below. Write the words in the blank. Try to complete the exercise without looking at the Vocabulary List in each lesson.

1. **Ecology Vocabulary** _____

2. **Vocabulary for Villains** _____

3. **A Question of Value** _____

4. **"Wild" Vocabulary** _____

5. **Beyond the Notes** _____

6. **Latin and Greek Roots** _____

7. **Taking a Stand** _____

8. **Food Vocabulary** _____

9. **Vocabulary for Law** _____

10. **"Perseverance" Vocabulary** _____

11. **Ancient Civilizations** _____

12. **Size and Shape** _____

13. **Vocabulary for "Hard Times"** _____

14. **Science Vocabulary** _____

15. **Number Prefixes** _____

symphony
migrate
trimester
premium
artifact
turbulent
habitat
circumstance
salvation
calamity
melodious
magnitude
insoluble
benign
menace
denounce
retort
bland
optimism
indulge
corrupt
bisect
verdict
diminish
endeavor
forte
anthropology
elongate
metamorphosis
destitute

Word Maps

You can draw a **word map** to help you understand what a word means and remember how to use it in context. The word map below is for a vocabulary word in this book.

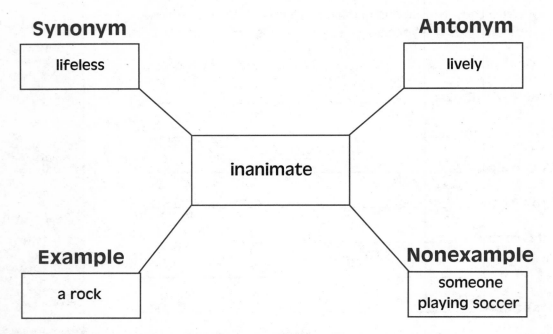

Synonym
lifeless

Antonym
lively

inanimate

Example
a rock

Nonexample
someone playing soccer

Vocabulary Word Used in an Example Sentence: *A rock is an inanimate object.*

A **Venn diagram** can help you compare and contrast two words. To complete a Venn diagram, write the features the words share where the circles overlap. In the outer part of each circle, write the features only that word has. You can also include examples of each word.

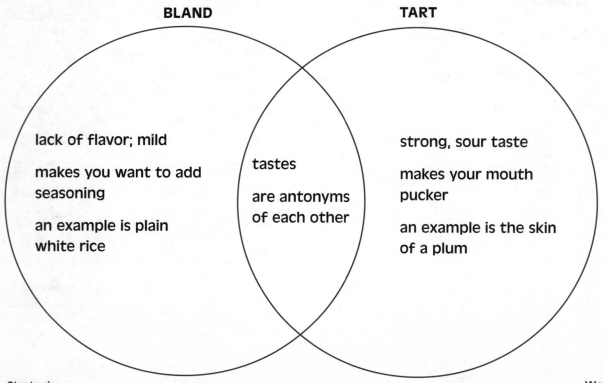

BLAND

TART

lack of flavor; mild

makes you want to add seasoning

an example is plain white rice

tastes

are antonyms of each other

strong, sour taste

makes your mouth pucker

an example is the skin of a plum

Categorization

A **category** is a kind of group. By placing words into categories, you can see how they are related, which will help you remember their meanings. The list below includes words that do not seem to be related.

edit	slant	tyrant
reformer	mentor	lyrics
melodious	publish	chaperon
retract	client	libel
opera	symphony	quintet

Here is the same list of words organized into categories.

Writing	**People**	**Music**
edit	mentor	lyrics
publish	chaperon	opera
retract	client	symphony
libel	tyrant	melodious
slant	reformer	quintet

To help even more, you can add the definitions of the words in each category to help you remember how they relate to the category's theme.

Writing

edit: to prepare written material for publication

publish: to prepare printed material to be sold or distributed to the public

retract: to take back a statement given orally or in writing

libel: a written statement that damages a person by questioning his or her character

slant: to present a point of view in writing that unfairly favors one side of an issue

Context Clues

Context clues are words, phrases, and sentences that tell something about an unknown word that you encounter in your reading. Sometimes context clues clearly tell a word's meaning, but other times they only hint at it.

Steps for Using Context Clues

1. Identify the unknown word.
2. List the words or phrases that tell something about its meaning.
3. Reread the sentence that contains the unknown word, and list clues found in that sentence. If you need more clues, reread the sentences before and after the one that contains the unknown word and, list those clues.
4. Guess the meaning of the unknown word based on your list of clues.

The following is a list of some types of context clues.

Definition Context Clues

The definition, or meaning, of an unknown word might be in the sentence or nearby sentences.

The *valiant*, or brave, knight saved the village from disaster.

Valiant means "brave" or "courageous."

Clue Words: *or, in other words, that is, which is, which means*

Example Context Clues

The meaning of an unknown word might be explained through examples.

Some people like to read *tabloids* such as *The National Enquirer* and *The Globe*.

The National Enquirer and *The Globe* are examples of *tabloids*. A *tabloid* is a short newspaper that prints sensational stories.

Clue Words: *for example, for instance, including, like, such as*

Context Clues

Cause-and-Effect Context Clues

An unknown word might be explained as part of a cause-and-effect relationship.

Because the concert was *monotonous*, I fell asleep.

The *monotonous concert* is the cause, and *falling asleep* is the effect. You can tell from the sentence that *monotonous* means "tiresome or uninteresting due to a lack of variety."

Clue Words: *as a result, because, consequently, therefore, thus*

Comparison Context Clues

An unknown word might be compared to a word or phrase that has the same meaning.

Isabella's mother thought her room was *filthy*. Her father, too, thought it was dirty.

Filthy and *dirty* have about the same meaning. In the sentences above, Isabella's mother and father thought the room looked the same.

Clue Words: *also, same, resembling, identical, similarly, too, likewise, like*

Contrast Context Clues

An unknown word might be contrasted with another word or phrase.

***Anthropologists* study human cultures; however, archaeologists dig up the remains of past human lives.**

An *anthropologist* and an *archaeologist* are both scientists, but they have different jobs.

Clue Words: *however, but, instead of, on the other hand, on the contrary, unlike*

General Context Clues

Sometimes there are not specific clues in a sentence to help you figure out the meaning of an unknown word. In this case, you can use the details in the words or sentences surrounding the unknown word; this is called using the general context.

The mountain climber went on a *rigorous* journey. She was alone, it was snowing, and the mountain she had to climb was 2,000 feet high.

The first sentence tells you that the mountain climber is going on some type of journey. The second sentence describes the details of the journey that would be considered *rigorous*, or *harsh*.

Word Relationships

Synonyms

A **synonym** is a word that has the same, or nearly the same, meaning as another word. *Speak* and *converse* are synonyms. The following sentences have the same meaning:

The student had to *speak* with the principal.
The student had to *converse* with the principal.

It is important to keep in mind that there are not many true synonyms, or words that have exactly the same meaning. Be careful when choosing a synonym because its shade of meaning might make a difference in your writing. For example, *happy* and *ecstatic* are synonyms, but *ecstatic* actually means "extremely excited."

Antonyms

An **antonym** is a word that has the opposite meaning of another word. *Spotless* and *filthy* are antonyms because *spotless* means something that is not at all dirty, and *filthy* means something that is extremely dirty. Sometimes the antonym of a word will appear in the same sentence. In the sentence below, *terminate* and *begin* are antonyms.

Even though the baseball players were ready to *begin* after the rain delay, the officials decided to *terminate* the game because there was a thunderstorm nearby.

Connotation

Connotation is the feeling associated with a word and can change the meaning of a sentence. A word can have a positive, negative, or neutral connotation. For example, *valiant* has a positive connotation because it is associated with being brave or impressive; *banish* has a negative connotation because it is associated with doing something bad and not being allowed to return. *Organism* has a neutral connotation because it does not have a more positive or negative feeling associated with it; it just means "a living thing."

When using a thesaurus to find synonyms, you should look up the synonyms in a dictionary if you are not familiar with them. That way you can make sure you use the word with the correct connotation. One way to figure out a word's connotation is to study an example sentence included with the definition of a word.

Word Relationships

Analogies

An **analogy** compares the relationships between two sets of words. Analogies, once they are completed, look like this:

>   *tennis* : *racquet* :: *golf* : *putter*   **-or-**   *initiate* is to *terminate* as *live* is to *perish*

Analogies often appear on tests. Analogy questions ask you to solve one half of the analogy and may appear in the following format:

TENNIS: RACQUET ::	**-or-**	*Initiate* is to *terminate* as _____ is to *perish*.
a. football : player		a. stop
b. golf : putter		b. begin
c. coach : team		c. live
d. player : equipment		d. jump

In the first example analogy, the single colon means "is related to" and the double colon means "as." So, the analogy is read, "Tennis is related to racquet as golf is related to putter." You can see that the analogy compares sports and their equipment. The second example analogy compares pairs of antonyms. You should use your knowledge of relationships between words to solve an analogy. Then you will be able to determine which word correctly completes the second pair.

Here are some other types of analogies:

Synonym Analogies

The words in each pair are synonyms.

deteriorate : worsen :: potent : powerful

Cause-and-Effect Analogies

The first word in each pair is the cause, and the second word is the effect.

inflammation : pain :: tornado : destruction

Part-Whole Analogies

The first word in each pair is part of the second word.

lyrics : song :: Earth : universe

Object-Use Analogies

The first word in each pair is an object, and the second word tells what you do with it.

beret : wear :: croissant : eat

Word Relationships

Homographs

Homographs are words that are spelled the same but have different meanings and sometimes different pronunciations.

> **I was called a *rebel* because I wanted to *rebel* against the unjust government.**
> **If the judge is *fair*, then our apple pie will win first prize at the county *fair*.**

When you are not sure you are using the right homograph, use a dictionary to check the meaning of the word.

Homophones

Homophones are words that have the same pronunciation but have different meanings and usually different spellings.

> **She gave her friend a *compliment* because her shoes were a good *complement* to her dress.**
> **The *principal* taught us a very important *principle*.**

Other homophones include *in/inn, gnu/knew/new, foul/fowl, rain/reign/rein, stair/stare, plain/plane, stationary/stationery,* and *their/there/they're*.

Related Words

Related words are words that have the same root word or base word. The way that words are related may be difficult to see, but if you break the word into parts, you can see how one word is related to another.

> **habitual:** doing something without having to think about it
> **inhabitant:** a person or animal that lives permanently in a place
> **habitat:** a place where plants and animals live

All three words above contain the word *habit*, which gives you a clue that they are related, but their meanings are different. *Habit* means "an act performed regularly."

Building Vocabulary Skills
Notebook Reference

To Reinforce Vocabulary Skills

Tools and Reference

Table of Contents

www.sra4kids.com

Send all inquiries to:
SRA/McGraw-Hill
8787 Orion Place
Columbus, OH 43240-4027

Printed in the United States of America.

R00004414

1 2 3 4 5 6 7 8 9 QPD 07 06 05 04 03 02

Columbus, OH • Chicago, IL • Redmond, WA

The McGraw-Hill Companies

Word Origins

The study of where, when, and how words originated is called *etymology*. Many English words come from words that were first used in ancient Rome where people spoke Latin. English words also come from other languages, such as Greek, French, German, and Spanish.

If you want to find out where a word originally came from, you do not have to look far. Entries in most collegiate dictionaries provide the origins of words and the date the word was first used in the English language. An entry that includes the origin of the word will look like this:

> **ap a thy** /ap′ ə thē/ *n.* [Greek, *apatheia,* from *apathēs* without feeling, from *a-* + *pathos* emotion] (1603) **1.** lack of feeling or emotion **2.** lack of interest or concern.

This dictionary entry tells you that *apathy* was first used in English in 1603 and came from words in Greek. Knowing the origin of words like *apathy* will sometimes help you figure out the meanings of unfamiliar words that you come across in your reading.

The next dictionary entry shows how the word *monopoly* came from two languages.

> **mo nop o ly** /mə nop′ ə lē/ *n.* [Latin, *monopolium,* from Greek *monōpolion,* from *mon-* + *pōlein* to sell] (1534) **1.** the exclusive control of something, such as manufactured goods or a service, by a person, group, or company. **2.** the right or privilege of such control granted by a government.

The entry above tells you that *monopoly* came from Greek and Latin, and that its first recorded use in English was in 1534.

Prefixes and Suffixes

Prefixes

Prefixes are added to the beginning of base words or root words to make new words.

Prefix	Meaning	Prefix	Meaning
bi-	two	*mis-*	wrong
cent-	one hundred	*mono-*	one
co-	together	*multi-*	many
con-	with	*non-*	not
contra-	against	*over-*	too much
de-	not; opposite	*pre-*	before
dis-	not; opposite	*re-*	again; back
ex-	former	*sub-*	under
in-, im-	into	*super-*	above
in-, im-, ir-, il-	not	*trans-*	across
inter-	among; between	*tri-*	three
mill-	one thousand	*un-*	not

Some vocabulary words from this book that have prefixes are *unpredictable, inanimate, displace, conform, trilogy, monorail,* and *millennium.*

Suffixes

Suffixes are added to the end of base words or root words to make new words.

Suffix	Meaning	Suffix	Meaning
-able, -ible	is; can be	*-ion*	state or quality of
-ance, -ence	state or quality of	*-ish*	relating to
-ant, -ent	one who	*-ist*	one who practices
-ary	place for	*-ity*	state or quality of
-er, -or	one who	*-ive*	inclined to
-ess	one who (female)	*-less*	without
-est	most	*-ly*	resembling
-ful	full of	*-ment*	action or process
-ial, -ian	relating to	*-ous*	full of
-ify	make; form into	*-y*	being; having

Some vocabulary words from this book that have suffixes are *ratification, melodious, publicity, predator, cosmologist, existence,* and *expansive.*

Roots

A **root** is the main part of word. Although a root may not be a word by itself, some forms can stand alone. Roots that can stand alone are called *base words.*

Prefixes and suffixes can be added to a root to make different words, but the root carries the main meaning of the word. For example, by itself the root *form* means "shape," but it can become *transform, reform,* or *deform* by adding a prefix. Also, it can become *transformation, reformer,* or *deformity* by adding a suffix. Below are lists of roots that come from the Greek and Latin languages.

Greek Roots

Root	Meaning	Words
anthr	man	anthropology
arch	ruler	monarchy
bio	life	biography
chron	time	chronological
cosm	universe	cosmic
geo	earth	geologist
hydr	water	dehydrate
meter	measure	centimeter
morph	form	metamorphosis
path	disease; feeling	pathetic
phon	sound	symphony

Latin Roots

Root	Meaning	Words
bene	good; well	beneficial
card	heart	cardiac
dic	speak	contradict
form	shape	conform
fort	strong	fortify
jus	law	justification
liber	free	liberation
mal	bad	maladjusted
mort	death	immortal
ped	foot	pedestrian

Chinese and Japanese Words

The English language has borrowed many words from other languages, including Chinese and Japanese. The words in the following lists are words that are used in Chinese and Japanese conversations. Be aware that when these words are written in Chinese or Japanese, they may look different because both languages use characters, which represent sounds and meanings, instead of letters.

Chinese Words

china   a fine pottery that is used for dishes and vases

chow   food

gung ho   very enthusiastic; eager

kowtow   to kneel and touch the forehead to the ground to show deep respect

tea   a drink made from dried and prepared leaves

tofu   a soft, white food made from mashed soybeans used in vegetarian cooking

typhoon   a tropical hurricane that occurs in the western Pacific Ocean

Japanese Words

bonsai   a miniature plant

hibachi   a small grill used to cook food

honcho   a person who is in charge

judo   a sport that emphasizes the use of quick movement and leverage to throw an opponent

karate   a system of unarmed self-defense

origami   the art of forming paper into objects

sayonara   goodbye

tycoon   a wealthy, powerful person in business

Figurative Language

You can use **figurative language** to make your writing or speech more interesting. Common types of figurative language are shown below.

Similes and Metaphors

Similes compare two unlike things by using the words *like* or *as*.

I watched the little girl flit around the garden *like* a butterfly.

Metaphors compare two unlike things *without* using the words *like* or *as*.

The little girl was a butterfly flitting around the garden.

Idioms

An **idiom** is an expression that cannot be understood by the meanings of the individual words within it. It is often a well-known saying or proverb whose original meaning is not well known. Understanding idioms will help you better understand what you read. For example, the idiom *down to the wire* means "undecided until the end" or "at the last minute." This phrase originally referred to races in which the winner is determined by whoever crosses the finish line first. A string is stretched across the finish to help the judges see clearly who crosses first in a close race. That string is called the *wire,* and the winner is the one who breaks the wire first.

Other common idioms include *a piece of cake,* which means "easy," *down in the dumps,* which means "sad and discouraged," *cold feet,* which means "nervousness," and *in the same boat,* which means "in the same situation."

Slang

Slang is speech that is normally not used in formal writing, but is used often when speaking, especially with friends. Some examples are *guys, dough,* and *bad,* which are slang for *people, money,* and *good,* respectively. Slang is frequently used as a shortcut and can vary from group to group. Three things can happen to slang:

1. It dies out and is no longer used.
2. It continues to survive as slang over a long period of time.
3. It becomes accepted as standard language.

Reference Skills

Thesaurus

A **thesaurus** lists synonyms, and usually antonyms, of words. For example, if you need to find another word that means *handsome,* a thesaurus might list the following synonyms: *good-looking, debonair, dignified.* You could substitute one of these words for *handsome,* but if you are not familiar with one of the words, you should look it up in the dictionary to make sure it will not change the meaning of your sentence.

Electronic Thesaurus

You will find an **electronic thesaurus** in most word-processing programs for computers. Most electronic thesauruses are similar to print thesauruses. To find synonyms for a word, simply highlight the word and then click on the thesaurus. The thesaurus will list synonyms and sometimes antonyms. It also sometimes includes brief definitions of words and tells which part of speech each meaning is. An electronic thesaurus entry will look similar to this:

Word looked up:	Replace with synonym:
verdict	*decision*
	judgment
	ruling
	decree

As when using a traditional thesaurus, the meanings of synonyms found in an electronic thesaurus should be double-checked in a dictionary.

Dictionary of Quotations

A **dictionary of quotations** lists quotes said by various people. You can look up quotes in a quotation dictionary in a number of different ways, including looking up the words in the quotation, the general subject of the quotation, or the person who said the quotation. A dictionary of quotations is a useful tool when you want to include a quote in an essay or speech to make it more interesting.

Rhyming Dictionary

A **rhyming dictionary** lists common words that rhyme. For example, if you are trying to write a poem and need to find a word that rhymes with *bound,* you might look in a rhyming dictionary and find words like *ground, sound, pound,* or *mound.* Rhyming dictionaries are also located on the Internet, so you can quickly search for rhyming words.

Reference Skills

The Parts of a Dictionary Entry

This is a complete dictionary entry, as it would appear in a college dictionary. Some dictionary entries may not include *all* of the information show in this sample entry.

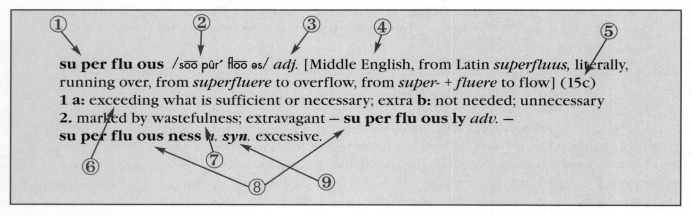

1. **Entry Word with Syllabication** – shows how to spell the word and how many syllables the word has

2. **Phonetic Spelling** – shows how to say the word

3. **Part of Speech** – shows the part of speech, which tells you how to use the word in a sentence

4. **Word Origin** – tells where the word was first used

5. **Date of First Use in English** – tells when the word was first used in the English language (*c* means "century")

6. **Most Common Definition** – gives the definition that is used most often in English

7. **Other Definitions** – gives other definitions, or multiple meanings, for the word

8. **Other Forms** –shows other forms of the word

9. **Synonym** – gives one or more synonyms for the word

Most dictionaries leave out the word origin and the date of first use in their entries. If abbreviations are used in a dictionary entry, there should be a list of abbreviations used in the dictionary either near the beginning or ending of the dictionary.

Parts of Speech

Nouns

Nouns name everything. For example, nouns name persons, places, things (this includes animals), and ideas. *Cat, mother, table, cafeteria,* and *happiness* are all nouns.

Pronouns

Pronouns can replace a noun or nouns so you do not have to keep repeating the noun or nouns you have already mentioned. For example, *her* and *she* are the pronouns in the following sentence: *Jennifer had to put on* her *coat because* she *was cold.*

Verbs

Verbs show action, state of being, or ownership. *Read* is a verb that shows action. *Is* is a verb because it shows state of being. *Have* is a verb that shows ownership. Verbs can change form to show time. For example, *she is tired* is in the present, but *she was tired* is in the past.

Adjectives

Adjectives describe nouns or pronouns. Adjectives usually answer one of the following questions: *What kind? Which one? How much? How many? Fortunate, silly, gnarled,* and *scandalous* are all adjectives.

Adverbs

Adverbs modify adjectives, verbs, or other adverbs. Adverbs usually answer one of the following questions: *When? Where? How? Why? Under what conditions? To what extreme?* The adverbs are italicized in the following phrases: *extremely* beautiful, walks *swiftly,* chews *very slowly.*

Prepositions

Prepositions show the relationship of nouns or pronouns to other words in a sentence: *We did not want to run* through *the puddle. They drove* across *the United States.*

Conjunctions

Conjunctions connect words or simple sentences to each other: *They wanted to go to the movies,* but *they did not have any money. I forgot my speech* because *I was nervous.*

Interjections

Interjections express surprise or emotion and usually stand alone. *Oh, wow,* and *ah* are interjections.

Glossary

A

ac com plish ment /ə kom′ plish mənt/ *n.* the successful completion of something; achievement. *Sending the first human into space was a great accomplishment.*

ac cu mu late /ə kū′ myə lāt′/ *v.* **accumulates, accumulating, accumulated.** to collect; to gather or pile up. *The mail often accumulates on my kitchen table all week.*

ac quaint ance /ə kwān′ təns/ *n.* **1.** a person one knows, but who is not a close friend. *I have two good friends and many acquaintances.* **2.** knowledge of something gained from experience. *She has an acquaintance with Alaska from her travels.*

ad he sive /ad hē′ siv/ *n.* a sticky substance. *Be sure to use the right adhesive when you glue that broken plate.* *adj.* having a sticky surface that holds to other things. *Some tape has two adhesive sides.*

ad o les cent /ad′ ə les′ ənt/ *n.* a person between childhood and adulthood, especially one between the ages of twelve and eighteen. *Adolescents learn to drive around the age of fifteen.*

af flic ted /ə flik′ tid/ *v.* **afflict.** to cause mental or physical pain; to severely suffer. *People all over the world were afflicted with a severe flu in 1918.*

a gent /ā′ jənt/ *n.* **1.** a person or company that has the power to act for others. *Our real estate agent represented us when we negotiated the sale of the house.* **2.** something that produces a certain effect. *Natural cleaning agents can be found in some stores.* **3.** an officer of a government agency. *CIA agents gather information about other countries.*

am ple /am′ pəl/ *adj.* **1.** more than enough. *There is ample food for our guests this weekend.* **2.** large in size; roomy. *Our guest bedroom has an ample closet.*

an thro pol o gy /an′ thrə pol′ ə jē/ *n.* the science of human cultures. *Cultural, or social, anthropology focuses on the customs and structure of human society.*

ap a thy /ap′ ə thē/ *n.* a lack of feeling or interest. *Political apathy disappeared during World War II.*

ap peal /ə pēl′/ *v.* **appeals, appealed.** **1.** to take a lower court's decision to a higher court to be heard again. *The defendant can appeal the jury's decision.* **2.** to make an earnest request. *Mary appealed to her parents to increase her allowance.* *n.* **1.** a legal action that brings a case to a higher court for review. *If you do not like the jury's decision, you can prepare an appeal.* **2.** an earnest request or call for help or sympathy. *I heard the lost child's appeal for help.* **3.** the power to attract or charm. *For Mom, washing dishes has no appeal.* *adj.* **appealing.** attractive, charming, or interesting. *Her new idea is the most appealing proposal to date.*

ap praise /ə prāz′/ *v.* **appraises, appraising, appraised.** **1.** to estimate the value of; to set a price for. *Real estate agents appraise land and homes.* **2.** to judge the quality or worth of. *A biographer must be able to appraise the character of the person who is the subject of a biography.*

ar chae ol o gy /är′ kē ol′ ə jē/ *n.* the scientific study of remains of past human life. *People working in the field of archaeology often go on digs to unearth fossils and other ancient materials.*

a ro ma /ə rō′ mə/ *n.* a pleasant odor; a fragrance. *The aroma of the Thanksgiving turkey baking in the oven brought everyone into the kitchen.*

ar ti fact /är′ tə fakt′/ *n.* a product of human skill. *Egyptian artifacts might include jewelry and tools from thousands of years ago.*

as ser tive /ə sûr′ tiv/ a form of **assert.** *adj.* bold; forward in manner. *Assertive people stand up for themselves.*

au dac i ty /ô das′ i tē/ *n.* **1.** boldness or daring. *Her audacity led the reporter to talk to the criminals in prison.* **2.** shameless boldness. *How could you have the audacity to walk into the president's office without an appointment?*

au di tion /ô dish′ ən/ *n.* a short demonstration of a performer's ability; a tryout. *The singer landed an audition for a New York show.*

B

ban ish /ban′ ish/ *v.* **banishes, banishing, banished. 1.** to force to leave; to exile. *The king wanted to banish the corrupt knight from his lands forever.* **2.** to drive away. *I banished from my mind the thought of failing the test.*

bar bar ic /bär bar′ ik/ *adj.* uncivilized or savage. *Barbaric forms of punishment for prisoners are no longer legal in this country.*

bar ter /bär′ tər/ *v.* **barters, bartering, bartered.** to trade things for other things without using money. *Early American colonists bartered grain for blankets with Native Americans.*

ben e dic tion /ben′ i dik′ shən/ *n.* a blessing. *As best man in the wedding, Tom included a benediction for the couple at the end of his speech.*

be nev o lence /bə nev′ ə ləns/ *n.* kindness; goodwill. *The acts of benevolence by the charity organization represented the efforts of many volunteers.*

be nign /bi nīn′/ *adj.* **1.** gentle and kind. *The librarian at our school has a benign smile.* **2.** not harmful. *The effect of the disease turned out to be completely benign.*

be ret /bə rā′/ *n.* a soft cap without a brim. *Many models were wearing black berets in the fashion show.*

bi lin gual /bī ling′ gwəl/ *adj.* **1.** speaking or writing two languages. *A bilingual person speaks two languages easily and fluently.* **2.** written or expressed in two languages. *A good bilingual dictionary is helpful when learning another language.*

bi o log i cal /bī ə loj′ i kəl/ *adj.* having to do with living organisms; relating to biology. *The biological experiment discovered new ways to help animals live longer.*

bi ped /bī′ ped/ *n.* a two-footed animal. *Birds are bipeds, but dogs have four feet.*

bi sect /bī′ sekt/ *v.* **bisects, bisecting, bisected.** to divide into two equal parts. *You can bisect an angle by drawing a straight line through the middle of it.*

bland /bland/ *adj.* **1.** mild in taste. *The doctor told my uncle to follow a very bland diet.* **2.** lacking excitement or distinction. *This is an interesting tale, but that is a bland story.*

blurt /blûrt/ *v.* **blurts, blurting, blurted.** to say suddenly or without thinking. *I try to think through a response and not blurt out a quick comment.*

bound /bound/ *v.* **bounds, bounding, bounded. 1.** to leap; spring. *The deer bounded into the forest.* **2.** to spring back after hitting something. *The basketball bounded off the rim of the net.*

/a/	at
/ā/	late
/â/	care
/ä/	father
/e/	set
/ē/	me
/i/	it
/ī/	kite
/o/	ox
/ō/	rose
/ô/	brought
	raw
/oi/	coin
/o͝o/	book
/o͞o/	too
/or/	form
/ou/	out
/u/	up
/yo͞o/	cube
/ûr/	turn
	germ
	learn
	firm
	work
/ə/	about
	chicken
	pencil
	cannon
	circus
/ch/	chair
/hw/	which
/ng/	ring
/sh/	shop
/th/	thin
/ᵗh/	there
/zh/	treasure

bu reau /byo͞or´ ō/ *n., pl.* **bureaus.**
1. a government department or office. *The Federal Bureau of Investigation investigates federal crimes.* 2. an office or agency. *We went to a travel bureau to make our vacation reservations.* 3. a chest of drawers. *My aunt gave me a white bureau for storing my clothes.*

C ━━━━━━━━━━━━━━━━━━━

ca lam i ty /kə lam´ i tē/ *n., pl.* **calamities.** a disastrous event causing pain and sorrow. *Fires and floods are examples of calamities.*

car di ac /kär´ dē ak´/ *adj.* of or relating to the heart. *Many hospitals have a cardiac unit to treat patients with heart problems.*

cen ten ni al /sen ten´ ē əl/ *n.* a hundredth anniversary of an event or the celebration of that anniversary. *Founded in 1776, the United States had its centennial in 1876.*

chant /chant/ *n.* a singing or shouting of words over and over. *Chants often have a strong rhythm. v.* **chants, chanting, chanted.** to sing or shout words over and over. *The crowd chanted the candidate's political slogan.*

chap er on /shap´ ə rōn´/ *n.* an older person who watches and supervises young people. *My aunt was one of the chaperons at the school dance.*

chron o log i cal /kron´ ə loj´ i kəl/ *adj.* in time order; arranged according to the order in which events happened. *A chronological table of inventions of the twentieth century might list first the phonograph developed by Thomas Edison.*

cir cu late /sûr´ kyə lāt´/ *v.* **circulates, circulating, circulated.** 1. to move freely. *The air circulates now that the window is open.* 2. to move in a circular course back to a starting point. *Water is conserved in some fountains because the same water circulates.*

cir cum stance /sûr´ kəm stans´/ *n.* a condition or an event related to other conditions or events. *The beautiful weather was a circumstance that made the holiday parade successful. pl.* **circumstances.** the state of affairs surrounding a person or action. *Our circumstances improved when we moved, found better jobs, and adopted a dog.*

civ ics /siv´ iks/ *n.* a study of the duties, rights, and privileges of citizens in relation to their government. *The word civics is plural, but it is used with a singular verb. Civics was the class in which we discussed the history of income tax.*

clam my /klam´ ē/ *adj.* cold and damp. *We opened the windows to air out the clammy basement.*

cli ché /klē shā´/ *n.* an overused saying or idea. *"You eat like a bird" is an example of a cliché.*

cli ent /klī´ ənt/ *n.* 1. a customer of a business. *The beauty salon's clients were happy when the salon was remodeled.* 2. a person or organization that uses the services of another person or organization. *That accounting firm's clients include Grandma, the orchestra, and a large charity.*

coax /kōks/ *v.* **coaxes, coaxing, coaxed.** to persuade or influence by gentle urging. *We coaxed the scared cat out from under the sofa.*

com mo tion /kə mō´ shən/ *n.* a noisy disturbance. *There was a commotion in the classroom when two dogs entered.*

com pat i ble /kəm pat´ ə bəl/ *adj.* able to exist together; well-suited. *Compatible roommates communicate well and do not fight.*

com pul so ry /kəm pul´ sə rē/ *adj.* required by law or rules. *Physical education classes are compulsory in the schools in our city.*

con densed /kən denst´/ *adj.* thickened. *Condensed milk is sweetened with sugar. v.* **condense, condensing, condensed.**

1. to thicken or reduce in volume. *In this recipe, condense the sauce by boiling it.* **2.** to shorten. *Please condense your paragraph from six to four sentences.* **3.** to change a gas to a liquid or a solid. *Vapor condenses overnight, taking the form of dew in the morning.*

con duc tor /kən duk′ tər/ *n.* **1.** a person who conducts or leads an orchestra. *Leonard Bernstein was a famous American conductor and composer.* **2.** a person on a train or bus who collects tickets. *The conductor walked through each car of the train asking for tickets.* **3.** a material or object that allows heat, electricity, or sound to flow easily. *Metal is a conductor of electricity.*

con fi den tial /kon′ fi den′ shəl/ *adj.* secret or private. *A confidential letter is meant to be seen only by the person to whom it is addressed.*

con form /kən form′/ *v.* **conforms, conforming, conformed. 1.** to behave or think in a way that agrees with a standard or a rule. *Students at our school conform to a dress code.* **2.** to be or make the same or similar. *These reports conform to the example in the textbook.*

con gre gate /kong′ gri gāt′/ *v.* **congregates, congregating, congregated.** to assemble; to come together in a crowd. *Many people congregated at the stadium entrance.*

con gru ent /kong′ grōō ənt/ *adj.* exactly the same in shape and size. *Congruent triangles have sides and angles that are exactly the same.*

con sci en tious /kon′ shē en′ shəs/ *adj.* careful and responsible; showing thought and care. *I made a conscientious effort to learn to speak German.*

con sen sus /kən sen′ səs/ *n.* a general agreement or opinion. *The consensus of the voters favored new school board elections.*

con stit u ent /kən stich′ ōō ənt/ *n.* **1.** a voter in a particular district. *The congressperson sent letters to all her constituents explaining her views.* **2.** a needed part. *Sand is a constituent of glass.*

con sum er /kən sōō′ mər/ *n.* a person who buys and uses up things offered for sale. *People who buy food, clothing, books, or other things are consumers.*

con ta gious /kən tā′ jəs/ *adj.* able to be spread from person to person. *Chicken pox is a contagious disease.*

con tem pla tion /kon′ təm plā′ shən/ *n.* deep and careful thought. *The president found time in his hectic schedule for some quiet contemplation.*

con tra dict /kon′ trə dikt′/ *v.* **contradicts, contradicting, contradicted.** to say the opposite of; to disagree with. *The nightly news contradicted earlier reports about the governor's possible resignation.*

con verse /kən vûrs′/ *v.* **converses, conversing, conversed.** to talk together. *My parents often converse in a funny, friendly way.*

cor ro sion /kə rō′ zhən/ *n.* the process of wearing away. *Rust was responsible for the corrosion on the old car.*

/a/	at
/ā/	late
/â/	care
/ä/	father
/e/	set
/ē/	me
/i/	it
/ī/	kite
/o/	ox
/ō/	rose
/ô/	brought
	raw
/oi/	coin
/ōō/	book
/ōō/	too
/or/	form
/ou/	out
/u/	up
/yōō/	cube
/ûr/	turn
	germ
	learn
	firm
	work
/ə/	about
	chicken
	pencil
	cannon
	circus
/ch/	chair
/hw/	which
/ng/	ring
/sh/	shop
/th/	thin
/ŧħ/	there
/zh/	treasure

cor rupt /kə rupt´/ *v.* **corrupts, corrupting, corrupted.** to cause to act badly or dishonestly; make rotten. *An older brother or sister can corrupt younger children in the family.* *adj.* dishonest and immoral; wicked. *The corrupt politician faced punishment for taking bribes.*

cos mo lo gist /koz mo´ lə jist/ *n.* a person who studies the makeup of the universe. *Amerigo Vespucci was a cosmologist of the fifteenth century.*

cos mos /koz´ mōs/ *n.* the universe considered as an ordered system. *Physicists such as Stephen Hawking have advanced our knowledge of the cosmos.*

cramped /krampt/ *adj.* a form of **cramp.** crowded, limited, or confined. *Submarines provide cramped living quarters for the onboard personnel.*

cri sis /krī´ sis/ *n.* **1.** a difficult time or situation. *The loss of his favorite toy caused a crisis for the toddler.* **2.** a decisive turning point. *That crisis intensified the nuclear arms race between the two nations.*

cri tic /krit´ ik/ *n.* **1.** someone who judges harshly; a faultfinder. *She heeds her supporters' advice, not her critics'.* **2.** person who has the job of reviewing books, movies, plays, and other artistic endeavors. *I always read my favorite critic's column in the newspaper before I see a play.*

cui sine /kwi zēn´/ *n.* **1.** a style of cooking or preparing food. *The cuisine of Italy uses a lot of tomatoes and garlic.* **2.** the food prepared, especially at a restaurant. *We like the Japanese cuisine at this restaurant.*

cy lin dri cal /sə lin´ dri kəl/ *adj.* a form of **cylinder.** shaped like a cylinder; long and round. *Cylindrical drums store oil and similar substances.*

cyn i cal /sin´ i kəl/ *adj.* having or showing doubt or disbelief about the sincerity of someone's actions. *The cynical reporter had trouble believing the teenagers' story.*

D

daw dle /dô´ dəl/ *v.* **dawdles, dawdling, dawdled.** to waste time. *Please do not dawdle on your way home from the store.*

deb o nair /deb´ ə nâr´/ *adj.* charming and pleasant. *Harrison Ford is a debonair movie star.*

de bris /də brē´/ *n.* the remains of something destroyed or broken; trash. *The crowd at the outdoor concert left a ton of debris on the field.*

de cree /di krē´/ *n.* **1.** an order or decision made by a court. *The divorce decree was announced in the newspapers.* **2.** any official decision. *The queen's decree raised taxes for repairs of historic buildings.* *v.* **decrees, decreeing, decreed.** to order or decide. *The president can decree a national holiday.*

de lin quent /di ling´ kwənt/ *adj.* **1.** failing in an obligation or duty. *Delinquent members will remit their dues payment next week.* **2.** due and not paid. *There is a penalty added to delinquent taxes.*

de nounce /di nouns´/ *v.* **denounces, denouncing, denounced.** **1.** to speak out against publicly; to object to. *That senator likes to denounce big business.* **2.** to accuse. *One of the thieves denounced his partner to the police.*

de plete /di plēt´/ *v.* **depletes, depleting, depleted.** to use up or reduce in amount. *The dancers' energy was depleted at the end of the recital.*

de prive /di prīv´/ *v.* **deprives, depriving, deprived.** **1.** to take away from. *The new parking garage deprived the community of its skating rink.* **2.** to keep from doing or having. *The corrupt ruler of that country is depriving its citizens of free elections.*

de scent /di sent´/ *n.* **1.** ancestry. *My family is of Swedish descent.* **2.** movement from a higher to a lower place. *We made a slow descent from the top of the canyon.*

des ti tute /des′ ti toot′/ *adj.* **1.** very poor; without the necessities of life. *Natural disasters may leave many people completely destitute.* **2.** totally lacking. *The empty desert appeared destitute of living creatures.*

de ter i or ate /di tir′ ē ə rāt′/ *v.* **deteriorates, deteriorating, deteriorated.** to make or become steadily worse. *The patient's condition deteriorated overnight.*

det ri men tal /det′ rə men′ təl/ *adj.* harmful; causing damage. *Lack of exercise can be detrimental to a person's health.*

dev as ta tion /dev′ ə stā′ shən/ *n.* an act or instance of destroying or ruining. *The fire caused almost total devastation of the forest area.*

de vour /di vour′/ *v.* **devours, devouring, devoured. 1.** to eat up greedily. *The boys devoured the food at the picnic after the softball game.* **2.** to destroy. *The flames of the fire devoured the cabin.* **3.** to enjoy greatly. *Young readers devour each book in the popular series.*

dig ni fied /dig′ nə fīd′/ *adj.* having or showing self-respect or self-control. *The actor possessed a very dignified manner on screen.*

di lute /di loot′/ *v.* **dilutes, diluting, diluted.** to thin or weaken with liquid. *If the soup is too thick, dilute it with a little water.*

di min ish /di min′ ish/ *v.* **diminishes, diminishing, diminished.** to make or become smaller or less. *The rainfall diminished by late afternoon.*

di min u tive /di min′ yə tiv/ *adj.* tiny; small in size. *A baby's fingers are quite diminutive.*

dip lo mat ic /dip′ lə mat′ ik/ *adj.* **1.** skilled with people. *A diplomatic person knows how to avoid hurting someone's feelings.* **2.** having to do with people who negotiate with foreign countries. *My brother plans to join the diplomatic service and travel.*

dis ci pline /dis′ ə plin/ *n.* training that develops skill, good character, or good behavior. *Good parents use discipline to show children how to live in the world. v.* **1.** to train to be obedient. *A drill sergeant disciplines new army recruits.* **2.** to develop or train. *I am trying to discipline my mind to ignore distractions while I do my homework.*

dis close /dis klōz′/ *v.* **discloses, disclosing, disclosed.** to make known. *Will you promise not to disclose my secret?*

dis cre tion /di skresh′ ən/ *n.* **1.** good judgment; caution. *The student showed discretion in reporting the accident to the proper authorities.* **2.** the freedom to act according to one's own judgment. *We left the selection of colleges to visit to our son's discretion.*

dis crim i na tion /di skrim′ ə nā′ shən/ *n.* **1.** unfair difference in treatment. *Discrimination on the basis of race or color is illegal in the United States.* **2.** the act of paying attention to small details. *The managing editor of the fashion magazine is a person of discrimination.*

dis mayed /dis mād′/ *v.* **dismay. 1.** to alarm or upset. *I was dismayed to find that my wallet was missing.* **2.** to discourage. *The voters' lack of support dismayed the new mayoral candidate.*

/a/	at
/ā/	late
/â/	care
/ä/	father
/e/	set
/ē/	me
/i/	it
/ī/	kite
/o/	ox
/ō/	rose
/ô/	brought
	raw
/oi/	coin
/oo/	book
/oo/	too
/or/	form
/ou/	out
/u/	up
/yoo/	cube
/ûr/	turn
	germ
	learn
	firm
	work
/ə/	about
	chicken
	pencil
	cannon
	circus
/ch/	chair
/hw/	which
/ng/	ring
/sh/	shop
/th/	thin
/ŧħ/	there
/zh/	treasure

dis place /dis plās´/ *v.* **displaces, displacing, displaced. 1.** to force to leave home or country. *Many families were displaced after the tornado destroyed their homes.* **2.** to take the place of. *Compact discs displaced audiocassettes as the most popular way to listen to music.*

dis tort /di stort´/ *v.* **distorts, distorting, distorted. 1.** to twist or bend out of shape. *The mirrors in a fun house distort the image of a person standing in front of them.* **2.** to change so as to be misleading. *Be careful not to distort the facts when you report the story.*

du ra tion /dŏŏ rā´ shən/ *n.* the length of time something continues or exists. *Despite the rain, the football fans stayed for the duration of the game.*

E

ed i ble /ed´ ə bəl/ *adj.* fit or safe to eat. *Some mushrooms found in the woods are not edible.*

ed it /ed´ it/ *v.* **edits, editing, edited. 1.** to correct and prepare for publication or presentation. *My mother edits manuscripts for a New York publishing company.* **2.** to review and cut for presentation. *Many movies are edited for television.*

e lon gate /i lông´ gāt/ *v.* **elongates, elongating, elongated.** to lengthen or stretch; to make longer. *Some women in Africa wear numerous tight metal necklaces to elongate their necks.*

e lu sive /i lōō´ siv/ *adj.* **1.** hard to catch or follow. *Spiders can be elusive insects.* **2.** hard to explain or understand. *The meaning of a poem can be elusive.*

en deav or /en dev´ ər/ *n.* a serious effort; attempt. *My endeavors at learning Chinese have not been very successful.* *v.* **endeavors, endeavoring, endeavored.** to try; to make an attempt. *I will endeavor to do better next term.*

e quiv a lent /i kwiv´ ə lənt/ *adj.* equal in value or meaning. *Nodding your head is equivalent to saying "yes."* *n.* something that is equal. *Four quarters are the equivalent of one dollar.*

e ro sion /i rō´ zhən/ *n.* a gradual wearing or washing away. *Many rock formations have been shaped by erosion over time.*

eth i cal /eth´ i kəl/ *adj.* moral; relating to standards of right and wrong. *It is not ethical to take someone else's words or ideas and pass them off as your own.*

e vap o rate /i vap´ ə rāt´/ *v.* **evaporates, evaporating, evaporated. 1.** to change from a liquid or solid into a vapor. *The dew evaporates into the warm air.* **2.** to disappear or fade away. *Our hopes for winning the game evaporated after the quarterback was injured.*

e volve /i volv´/ *v.* **evolves, evolving, evolved.** to develop slowly over time. *A star evolves from condensed clouds of gas and dust.*

ex ca va tion /eks´ kə vā´ shən/ *n.* the act or site of digging. *The excavation of the tomb of King Tutankhamen in 1922 was a historic event.*

ex ist ence /eg zis´ təns/ *n.* **1.** the condition of being real. *The existence of xenon gas in Earth's atmosphere was discovered in 1898.* **2.** life. *The existence of some Native American tribes was threatened by diseases carried by European settlers.*

ex pan sive /ek span´ siv/ *adj.* extending widely. *The expansive high plains of the United States are home to antelope.*

ex tinct /ek stingkt´/ *adj.* **1.** no longer existing. *The passenger pigeon has been extinct since 1914.* **2.** no longer burning or active. *Mt. Hood is an extinct volcano in northwest Oregon.*

F

fa tigue /fə tēg´/ *n.* exhaustion; loss of strength. *The delivery driver suffered from fatigue after driving the truck for eight hours in the snowy weather.*

filth y /fil´ thē/ *adj.* extremely dirty. *The children were filthy after playing in the mud.*

flail /flāl/ *v.* **flails, flailing, flailed.** to wave or swing violently. *The boy still flailed his arms even as the teacher broke up the fight.*

flit /flit/ *v.* **flits, flitting, flitted.** to dart about. *The hostess flitted through the room making sure the party guests had everything they needed.*

flux /fluks/ *n., pl.* **fluxes.** constant change or movement. *My summer vacation plans remained in a state of flux on July 4th.*

fo li age /fō´ lē ij/ *n.* the leaves on a tree or a plant. *Many people like to drive through New England in the fall to view the beautiful foliage.*

forte /fort/ *n.* a person's strong point. *My sister's forte is cooking gourmet meals.*

for ti fy /for´ tə fī´/ *v.* **fortifies, fortifying, fortified. 1.** to make stronger or more secure. *The scientist knew that his research would fortify his theory.* **2.** to protect with a wall, ditch, or other defense. *Fortify the castle by building high stone walls.*

for ti tude /for´ tə tōōd´/ *n.* courage or strength in the face of pain, danger, or misfortune. *The team of women who climbed Mt. Everest showed great fortitude.*

fra ter nal /frə tûr´ nəl/ *adj.* brotherly; relating to a brother or brothers. *The two friends had a fraternal relationship.*

fren zy /fren´ zē/ *n., pl.* **frenzies.** an outburst of great excitement or frantic activity. *The children were in a frenzy on the day before the start of winter break.*

G

garb /gärb/ *n.* clothing, especially of a distinctive type. *We could tell they were in the navy by their military garb.*

gnarled /närld/ *adj.* **1.** having many rough, twisted knots. *The old oak trees in the woods had gnarled trunks.* **2.** rough or rugged in appearance. *A farmer or construction worker often has gnarled hands.*

gour met /gŏŏr mā´/ *n.* an expert in choosing good food and drink. *My aunt is a gourmet who makes the best French food I have ever tasted.*

gruff /gruf/ *adj.* **1.** rough and unfriendly. *The doctor had a gruff manner, but we could tell that he was kind and caring.* **2.** harsh or hoarse. *The actor's gruff voice was his trademark.*

H

hab i tat /hab´ i tat´/ *n.* the place in which plants and animals naturally live. *The oceans of the world are the habitat of whales.*

hid e ous /hid´ ē əs/ *adj.* very ugly; horrible. *The cover of the science fiction book showed a hideous creature.*

hi er o glyph ics /hī´ ər ə glif´ iks/ *n. pl., sing.* **hieroglyphic.** picture symbols. *The hieroglyphics in the pyramid were studied by many scientists.*

/a/	at
/ā/	late
/â/	care
/ä/	father
/e/	set
/ē/	me
/i/	it
/ī/	kite
/o/	ox
/ō/	rose
/ô/	brought
	raw
/oi/	coin
/ŏŏ/	book
/ōō/	too
/or/	form
/ou/	out
/u/	up
/yōō/	cube
/ûr/	turn
	germ
	learn
	firm
	work
/ə/	about
	chicken
	pencil
	cannon
	circus
/ch/	chair
/hw/	which
/ng/	ring
/sh/	shop
/th/	thin
/th/	there
/zh/	treasure

hov er /huv′ ər/ *v.* **hovers, hovering, hovered.** to remain suspended in the air; to linger. *Helicopters can hover over the ground.*

hu mil i a tion /hyo͞o mil′ ē ā′ shən/ *n.* a feeling of embarrassment or shame. *Complete humiliation came over me when I dropped my lunch tray.*

I ▬▬▬▬▬▬▬▬▬▬▬▬

im mi nent /im′ ə nənt/ *adj.* about to happen. *The imminent storm made us pack up our picnic items and drive home.*

im mor tal /i môr′ təl/ *adj.* **1.** living forever. *Nothing on Earth is immortal.* **2.** famous or lasting through time. *Einstein's discoveries gave him immortal fame.*

in an i mate /in an′ ə mit/ *adj.* without life, unmoving. *Pyramids are inanimate structures.*

in dig na tion /in′ dig nā′ shən/ *n.* anger caused by something unjust or cruel. *The use of child labor in some countries arouses indignation in the rest of the world.*

in dis pen sa ble /in′ di spen′ sə bəl/ *adj.* absolutely necessary. *A good night's sleep is indispensable to feeling alert the next day.*

in dulge /in dulj′/ *v.* **indulges, indulging, indulged.** **1.** to allow oneself to enjoy something. *We indulged in an afternoon of reading in the park.* **2.** to give in to or yield to. *My mother says that my grandmother indulges us by giving us what we want.*

in fe ri or /in fir′ ē ər/ *adj.* **1.** of poor quality; below average. *The clothing in this discount store is inferior.* **2.** low or lower in quality or importance. *There is no reason for you to feel inferior to other people.*

in fir ma ry /in fûr′ mə rē/ *n.* a place for the care of the sick or injured. *My brother spent a week in the infirmary at boarding school after he broke his leg.*

in flam ma tion /in′ flə mā′ shən/ *n.* a condition of a part of the body with redness, swelling, and pain. *Inflammation is usually caused by an injury or infection.*

in gen ious /in jēn′ yəs/ *adj.* clever, inventive, or imaginative. *Virtual reality simulators are examples of ingenious technology.*

i ni ti ate /i nish′ ē āt′/ *v.* **initiates, initiating, initiated.** **1.** to begin or introduce. *Louis Pasteur initiated the practice of destroying bacteria in food.* **2.** to admit someone into an organization or club. *The Girl Scouts initiates girls up to age 17.*

in sig nif i cant /in′ sig nif′ i kənt/ *adj.* **1.** having little or no importance or meaning. *My mother told me never to worry about the insignificant things in life.* **2.** small in amount or size. *The amount of rainfall recorded that day was insignificant.*

in sol u ble /in sol′ yə bəl/ *adj.* **1.** unable to be dissolved. *Oil is insoluble in water.* **2.** unable to be solved. *Preventing crime seems to be an insoluble problem.*

in tense /in tens′/ *adj.* **1.** very great or strong; extreme. *The intense summer heat burned the green grass of our lawn.* **2.** having or showing strong feeling or effort. *The athlete's intense expression was an indication of her resolve to win the race.*

in ter de pen dent /in′ tər di pen′ dənt/ *adj.* dependent on one another. *The pioneers traded with Native Americans and were more interdependent than people today.*

in tu i tion /in′ to͞o ish′ ən/ *n.* a quick understanding about something without using conscious reasoning; a hunch. *The lawyer's intuition told her that the witness was not telling the truth.*

in vert ed /in vûrt′ id/ *adj.* a form of **invert.** **1.** reversed in position. *When dividing two fractions, multiply the dividend by the inverted divisor.* **2.** turned upside down. *Telescopes show inverted images of celestial objects.*

in vest ment /in vest′ mənt/ *n.* **1.** the use of money to make money. *Those people gain good returns from their investments.* **2.** the amount of money committed. *His investment in our business was several thousand dollars.* **3.** something into which money is put. *Real estate is usually a good investment.*

J

jo vi al /jō′ vē əl/ *adj.* merry or jolly. *Our jovial neighbor always smiles.*

jus ti fi ca tion /jus′ tə fi kā′ shən/ *n.* a satisfactory reason or explanation. *The student's constant lateness was justification for the phone call to his parents.*

L

lank y /lang′ kē/ adj. tall and thin. *A lanky person sometimes appears to be clumsy.*

li bel /lī′ bəl/ *n.* **1.** a false charge. *A person must be careful not to print libel about someone else.* **2.** the act or crime of damaging a person's reputation by publishing false information about him or her. *Newspapers and magazines have been sued for libel by movie stars.*

lib er a tion /lī′ bə rā′ shən/ *n.* the act or state of being set free; freedom. *The women's liberation movement of the 1960s sought to secure equal pay for women.*

lu na tic /lōō′ nə tik/ *n.* **1.** an insane person. *There are special public and private places for lunatics in our country.* **2.** a senseless or reckless person. *Only a lunatic would drive in this blizzard.*

lurch /lûrch/ *v.* **lurches, lurching, lurched.** to move suddenly in an unsteady manner. *The train lurched forward.*

lus cious /lush′ əs/ *adj.* smelling or tasting delicious. *The restaurant served a luscious variety of fruit for dessert.*

lyr ics /lir′ iks/ *pl. n.* the words of a song. *Timeless songs usually have well-known lyrics.*

M

mag ni tude /mag′ ni tūd′/ *n.* **1.** great size; size. *The magnitude of the Milky Way is enormous.* **2.** importance. *The invention of the electric lightbulb was a discovery of great magnitude.*

ma jor i ty /mə jôr′ i tē/ *n., pl.* **majorities.** the larger number or part of something; more than half. *The majority of students voted to continue the after-school reading club.*

ma lig nant /mə lig′ nənt/ *adj.* evil or harmful in nature or effect. *Dictatorships have a malignant influence on society.*

ma neu ver /mə nōō′ vər/ *v.* **maneuvers, maneuvering, maneuvered. 1.** to move skillfully or cleverly. *We should maneuver our way to the front of the crowd.* **2.** to cause soldiers or ships to move in a certain way. *The captain maneuvered the ships into position for the attack. n.* any strategic or clever move or plan. *The candidate's skillful political maneuvers will probably land him in the White House.*

me lo di ous /mə lō′ dē əs/ *adj.* pleasant to hear; musical. *We heard the melodious sounds of wind chimes from our back porch.*

/a/	at
/ā/	late
/â/	care
/ä/	father
/e/	set
/ē/	me
/i/	it
/ī/	kite
/o/	ox
/ō/	rose
/ô/	brought
	raw
/oi/	coin
/o͝o/	book
/o͞o/	too
/or/	form
/ou/	out
/u/	up
/yo͞o/	cube
/ûr/	turn
	germ
	learn
	firm
	work
/ə/	about
	chicken
	pencil
	cannon
	circus
/ch/	chair
/hw/	which
/ng/	ring
/sh/	shop
/th/	thin
/ th/	there
/zh/	treasure

men ace /men′ is/ *n.* **1.** a person or thing that is a threat or a danger. *Drunken drivers are a menace to society.* **2.** a pest or nuisance. *That raccoon has become a menace to the neighborhood.*

men tor /men′ tər/ *n.* a wise and trusted counselor. *A school guidance counselor is a mentor to students.*

met a mor pho sis /met′ ə môr′ fə sis/ *n.* **1.** the changes that certain animals go through as they develop. *Tadpoles become frogs through the process of metamorphosis.* **2.** a complete change of form. *When an ice cube goes through metamorphosis it can change into water or vapor.*

mi grate /mī′ grāt/ *v.* **migrates, migrating, migrated.** to move periodically from one region or country to another. *In the late fall, flocks of birds migrate to the warmer regions of the south.*

mil len ni um /mi len′ ē əm/ *n.* a period of a thousand years. *Many cities celebrated the millennium on December 31, 1999.*

mi nor i ty /mə nor′ i tē/ *n., pl.* **minorities. 1.** the smaller part of a group or whole; less than half. *A minority of citizens voted for the opposing mayoral candidate.* **2.** a group of people different from the larger group of which it is a part. *Minorities may be classified by nationality, politics, religion, or race.*

mo bi lize /mō′ bə līz′/ *v.* **mobilizes, mobilizing, mobilized.** to become organized. *My mother mobilizes the family before a long car trip.*

mon ar chy /mon′ ər kē/ *n.* a nation or state ruled by a hereditary ruler, such as a king or queen. *The American colonies used to be under control of the English monarchy.*

mon i tor /mon′ i tər/ *v.* **monitors, monitoring, monitored. 1.** to check, watch, or listen to. *We monitored the radio and television for more news about the disaster.* **2.** to supervise. *The town's police officers monitored the crowd at the downtown arts festival.* *n.* **1.** a student who has a special duty to perform. *The hall monitor made sure that no one wandered the halls.* **2.** a computer screen. *New computer monitors are much thinner than earlier models.*

mon o cle /mon′ ə kəl/ *n.* an eyeglass for one eye. *The monocle, introduced in England about 1800, was first called an "eye ring."*

mo nop o ly /mə nop′ ə lē/ *n., pl.* **monopolies. 1.** the sole control of something, such as a product or service, by a person or company. *A public utility may have a monopoly on services such as electricity.* **2.** a person or company that has sole control of something. *For a monopoly to exist, other companies cannot compete.*

mon o rail /mon′ ə rāl′/ *n.* **1.** a train that runs on a single rail. *The city of Seattle has a monorail.* **2.** a railroad track with one rail. *Train cars may be suspended beneath a monorail or they may run on the rail.*

mo not o nous /mə not′ ə nəs/ *adj.* tiring or uninteresting because it is unchanging. *Assembly line jobs are monotonous because workers do the same thing over and over.*

mon soon /mon soon′/ *n.* a seasonal wind of the Indian Ocean. *A monsoon blows from the land toward the ocean in winter.*

mon u ment /mon′ yə mənt/ *n.* a statue, building, or other structure made to honor a person or an event. *Mt. Rushmore National Memorial in South Dakota is a monument to four U.S. presidents.*

mo rale /mə ral′/ *n.* mental attitude or general spirit of a person or a group. *Morale was low after our school lost the spelling bee.*

O

op er a /op′ ər ə/ *n.* a play in which all or most of the words are sung. *The costumes and scenery were a grand background for the opera.*

op pres sive /ə pres′ iv/ *adj.* **1.** cruel and unjust. *The dictator was guilty of enforcing oppressive laws on his people.* **2.** causing difficulty or suffering. *The oppressive heat kept many elderly people inside.*

op ti mism /op′ tə miz′ əm/ *n.* hopefulness. *A sunny day always fills me with optimism.*

or deal /or dēl′/ *n.* a difficult or painful experience. *Climbing Mt. Everest is an ordeal for any climber.*

or di nance /or′ də nəns/ *n.* a city or town law. *Many towns have ordinances that make it illegal to litter on the streets and roads.*

or gan ism /ôr′ gə niz′ əm/ *n.* a living thing. *Many organisms can be seen only with a microscope.*

P

par al lel /par′ ə lel′/ *adj.* **1.** always an equal distance apart; never touching. *A globe is marked with parallel lines of latitude.* **2.** similar, alike. *The twins had lived apart for years but led parallel lives.*

pa thet ic /pə thet′ ik/ *adj.* **1.** arousing pity or sadness. *A wet kitten is a pathetic sight.* **2.** miserably inadequate. *The team made a pathetic attempt to score in the final minutes of the game.*

ped i gree /ped′ i grē′/ *n.* a line of ancestors. *Champion show dogs have good pedigrees.*

pe nal ize /pen′ ə līz′/ *v.* **penalizes, penalizing, penalized.** to give a penalty or punishment to. *The official penalized four hockey players during the third period.*

per ish /per′ ish/ *v.* **perishes, perishing, perished. 1.** to die. *Many people perished when the Titanic sank.* **2.** to disappear or vanish. *Abraham Lincoln stated that "government of the people, by the people, for the people, shall not perish from the earth."*

per pen dic u lar /pûr′ pən dik′ yə lər/ *adj.* **1.** at right angles. *Avenues in New York City run north and south and are perpendicular to the streets running east and west.* **2.** straight up and down. *The perpendicular face of the cliff was difficult for the group of climbers.*

per se ver ance /pûr′ sə vir′ əns/ *n.* determination; sticking to a goal. *The climbers' perseverance paid off when they reached the highest peak of the mountain range.*

pe tite /pə tēt′/ *adj.* small or tiny. *Dresses come in petite sizes.*

pet ri fy /pet′ rə fī′/ *v.* **petrifies, petrifying, petrified. 1.** to turn to stone. *Dead wood petrifies when water leaves minerals inside the wood cells.* **2.** to make helpless with fear or horror. *The scary movie petrified us when we saw it the first time.*

por tray /por trā′/ *v.* **portrays, portraying, portrayed. 1.** to describe; represent. *My favorite book portrays life in California in the nineteenth century.* **2.** to make a picture of someone or something. *The artist portrayed his hometown in a series of paintings.* **3.** to play the part of. *The actor portrayed President Truman in the movie.*

po tent /pō′ tənt/ *adj.* powerful; having strength and force. *The doctor told my mother to be careful to follow the prescribed dosage of the potent medicine.*

/a/	at
/ā/	late
/â/	care
/ä/	father
/e/	set
/ē/	me
/i/	it
/ī/	kite
/o/	ox
/ō/	rose
/ô/	brought, raw
/oi/	coin
/o͝o/	book
/o͞o/	too
/or/	form
/ou/	out
/u/	up
/yo͞o/	cube
/ûr/	turn, germ, learn, firm, work
/ə/	about, chicken, pencil, cannon, circus
/ch/	chair
/hw/	which
/ng/	ring
/sh/	shop
/th/	thin
/ᴛʜ/	there
/zh/	treasure

pred a tor /pred′ ə tər/ *n.* an animal that lives by hunting other animals for food. *Lions, hawks, and wolves are not plant eaters; they are predators.*

pre mi um /prē′ mē əm/ *n.* **1.** a high or unusual value. *My parents put a premium on honesty.* **2.** an amount paid for insurance. *Many companies pay the monthly insurance premiums for their employees.*

pre ten tious /pri ten′ shəs/ *adj.* making claims to, or presenting a false display of, some quality or importance. *The pretentious actress told reporters that she descended from royalty.*

prin ci ple /prin′ sə pəl/ *n.* **1.** a basic truth, belief, or law. *The United States was founded on the principle of separation of powers.* **2.** a rule of behavior that a person chooses to live by. *One of my principles is to always be kind to elderly persons.*

pro ce dure /prə sē′ jər/ *n.* a specific way of doing something. *The procedure for checking into the hotel required us first to give our name.*

pro claim /prə klām′/ *v.* **proclaims, proclaiming, proclaimed.** to announce publicly. *The warring countries proclaimed an end to their battle during the holidays.*

pub lic i ty /pu blis′ i tē/ *n.* **1.** information given out to bring a person or thing to public attention. *The publicity about the trial brought a large crowd to the courthouse.* **2.** public notice or attention. *Some famous people do not like publicity.*

pub lish /pub′ lish/ *v.* **publishes, publishing, published. 1.** to print a book, newspaper, or other material and offer it for sale. *This company publishes the best magazine in Europe.* **2.** to make generally known. *Please do not publish our family woes.*

punc tu al /pungk′ choo əl/ *adj.* on time. *We like to be punctual when we go to a concert.*

pun gent /pun′ jənt/ *adj.* sharp to the taste or smell. *Some kinds of mustard are pleasantly pungent.*

put ter /put′ ər/ *n.* a golf club with an upright head used for rolling the ball across the green. *The golfer carefully lined up the putter for his final shot.* *v.* **putters, puttering, puttered.** to work or act in an aimless way. *My father putters around his workshop in the basement on Saturdays.*

Q

qualify /kwol′ ə fī′/ *v.* **qualifies, qualifying, qualified. 1.** to meet the requirements; to be fit for something. *Her years of experience qualified her to become principal of the school.* **2.** to limit or restrict. *I had to qualify my statement that everyone loved chocolate with the word* almost.

quar an tine /kwor′ ən tēn′/ *v.* **quarantines, quarantining, quarantined.** to keep apart from others in order to prevent the spreading of a disease. *The children with the flu were immediately quarantined to keep the virus from spreading throughout the school.*

quib ble /kwib′ əl/ *v.* **quibbles, quibbling, quibbled.** to make minor objections or argue about something petty. *The parents quibbled about what to eat that night.*

quin tet /kwin tet′/ *n.* **1.** a group of five. *A quintet of managers led the workers in a cheer for meeting the monthly goals.* **2.** a musical group of five performers. *The members of the quintet all wore white shirts and black pants or skirts.*

quo ta /kwō′ tə/ *n.* a required amount or part due to or from a person or group. *Salespeople often have a quota of goods to sell each month.*

R

rat i fi ca tion /rat´ ə fi kā´ shən/ *n.* official or formal approval. *Special state conventions were set up for the ratification of the U.S. Constitution.*

ra tion /rash´ ən/ *n.* a definite or fixed amount, especially of food. *Each hiker carried a ration of food in his or her backpack. n. pl.* **rations.** food. *The soldiers received their rations for the day. v.* **rations, rationing, rationed.** to give out in portions. *Gasoline was rationed during the war years.*

re ac tor /rē ak´ tər/ *n.* a device used to produce atomic energy. *Nuclear reactors serve as valuable sources of electric power.*

re bel /ri bel´/ *v.* **rebels, rebelling, rebelled.** to resist or turn against. *Teenagers often try to rebel against authority. n.* **reb el** /reb´ əl/ **1.** a person who fights against authority. *The rebels attacked the dictator's palace.* **2. Rebel.** a soldier who fought against the North in the Civil War. *The Rebels in the Civil War won victories in 1861 and 1862.*

reck on /rek´ ən/ *v.* **reckons, reckoning, reckoned. 1.** to consider; to think. *She reckons that her friend is the best student in the class.* **2.** to count or calculate. *Sales tax is reckoned on the selling price of an item.*

rec on cile /rek´ ən sīl´/ *v.* **reconciles, reconciling, reconciled. 1.** to make friendly again. *After our argument, my friend and I quickly reconciled.* **2.** to become resigned to something. *We became reconciled to the fact that we were hopelessly lost.* **3.** to make agree. *The reporter had to reconcile the varying accounts of the robbery.*

re cur /ri kûr´/ *v.* **recurs, recurring, recurred.** to happen or appear again. *My grandmother's headache recurred every two days.*

re form er /ri form´ ər/ *n.* one who urges or brings about improvement. *Jane Addams was a social reformer who worked for justice for the poor.*

reg u late /reg´ yə lāt´/ *v.* **regulates, regulating, regulated. 1.** to manage or control by rule. *The Federal Reserve Board and other government agencies help regulate the U.S. economy.* **2.** to control or set. *The heart regulates the flow of blood throughout the body.*

re jec tion /ri jek´ shən/ *n.* refusal to accept or believe. *Our offer of help to our neighbors has always resulted in rejection.*

re ju ve nate /ri jōō´ və nāt´/ *v.* **rejuvenates, rejuvenating, rejuvenated.** to make young and energetic again. *Exercise rejuvenates the human body.*

rel e vant /rel´ ə vənt/ *adj.* appropriate; relating to what is being discussed. *Your question is not relevant to this discussion.*

re luc tant /ri luk´ tənt/ *adj.* unwilling; feeling hesitation. *She was reluctant to loan her brother more money.*

ren dez vous /rän´ də vōō´/ *n.* **1.** an appointment to meet at a certain place at a certain time. *We arranged a rendezvous at the restaurant at six p.m.* **2.** any meeting place. *Our usual rendezvous is the park on Saturday mornings. v.* **rendezvoused.** to meet by arrangement. *They will rendezvous at the east entrance to the mall at ten a.m. on Friday.*

/a/	at
/ā/	late
/â/	care
/ä/	father
/e/	set
/ē/	me
/i/	it
/ī/	kite
/o/	ox
/ō/	rose
/ô/	brought raw
/oi/	coin
/o͝o/	book
/o͞o/	too
/or/	form
/ou/	out
/u/	up
/yo͞o/	cube
/ûr/	turn germ learn firm work
/ə/	about chicken pencil cannon circus
/ch/	chair
/hw/	which
/ng/	ring
/sh/	shop
/th/	thin
/ th̷/	there
/zh/	treasure

rep re sent /rep´ ri zent´/ *v.* **represents, representing, represented. 1.** to stand for; to symbolize. *A large "H" on a highway sign represents a hospital.* **2.** to speak or act for. *An attorney represents a person in a court of law.*

rep u ta tion /rep´ yə tā´ shən/ *n.* the general opinion of a person or thing. *Lying to your friends will give you a bad reputation.*

res i due /rez´ i doō´ / *n.* remaining substance. *After we strained the tea leaves, we rinsed the residue from the metal strainer.*

re sume /ri zoōm´/ *v.* **resumes, resuming, resumed. 1.** to go on with after an interruption. *The play resumed after a brief intermission.* **2.** to take again; to return to. *We resumed our seats after giving the actress a standing ovation.*

re tort /ri tort´/ *v.* **retorts, retorting, retorted.** to reply quickly or sharply. *When reporters questioned him, the actor retorted, "I have no comment." n.* a quick or sharp reply. *My retort to her annoying statement was, "So what!"*

re tract /ri trakt´/ *v.* **retracts, retracting, retracted. 1.** to take back or withdraw. *The politician retracted his earlier statement.* **2.** to draw back in. *Cats retract their claws by instinct.*

re vive /ri vīv´/ *v.* **revives, reviving, revived. 1.** to bring back to consciousness. *The nurse revived the boy who had been knocked out by the baseball.* **2.** to bring back into use or interest. *She successfully revived several old plays on Broadway.* **3.** to give new strength to. *The ice-cold glasses of lemonade revived the tired walkers.*

ri gor ous /rig´ ər əs/ *adj.* harsh; very strict or severe. *Army basic training is a rigorous test for a young man or woman.*

rit u als /rich´ oō əlz/ *pl. n.* **1.** special customs and ceremonies. *The rituals of some families on Thanksgiving include a turkey dinner and watching football.* **2.** regular actions or procedures. *Walks and eating blueberry muffins are morning rituals in our family.*

ro bust /rō bust´/ *adj.* healthy and strong; vigorous or hardy. *The young swimmer had a robust appetite.*

S

sal va tion /sal vā´ shən/ *n.* the act of saving or the condition of being saved or rescued from something. *We seek salvation in music during the difficult times of our lives.*

sa vor /sā´ vər/ *v.* **savors, savoring, savored. 1.** to taste or smell with pleasure. *The guests savored the delicious meal served by the host.* **2.** to take great delight in. *The team members savored their victory long after the game ended.*

scan dal ous /skan´ də ləs/ *adj.* shocking; disgraceful. *Her scandalous behavior at the prom embarrassed everyone.*

scav en ger /skav´ ən jər/ *n.* **1.** an animal that feeds on decaying animals or plant matter. *The hyena is a scavenger.* **2.** a person who looks through trash for things that can be used or sold. *The scavenger found an old pan and a broken clock during his morning search.*

scoun drel /skoun´ drəl/ *n.* an evil or dishonest person. *In real life, Butch Cassidy was a thief and a scoundrel.*

scowl /skoul/ *v.* **scowls, scowling, scowled.** to frown angrily. *In a tense game, the coach often will be seen scowling on the sidelines. n.* an angry or sullen frown. *That scowl on your face will not be attractive in the family picture.*

self-ev i dent /self´ ev´ i dənt/ *adj.* obvious; needing no proof. *The fact that the road needed repairs was self-evident to us as we drove our car over all the potholes.*

se vere /sə vir´/ *adj.* **1.** strict; harsh. *The severe weather forecast made us decide to postpone our plan to go sailing.* **2.** serious;

critical. *Many severe illnesses such as polio have been virtually eliminated in modern times.*

si mul ta ne ous /sī′ məl tā′ nē əs/ *adj.* at the same time. *The divers made simultaneous dives off the high boards.*

skep ti cal /skep′ ti kəl/ *adj.* doubtful or disbelieving. *Helen Keller's parents were skeptical that their daughter could be taught to communicate.*

sketch y /skech′ ē/ *adj.* **1.** not complete. *The injured accident victim gave only a sketchy account of what happened.* **2.** not detailed or finished. *The sketchy drawings depicted a basic idea of the final product.*

slant /slant/ *v.* **slants, slanting, slanted. 1.** to present in a certain way. *The television reporter slanted the story toward the American audience.* **2.** to slope or lie at an angle. *The roofs of many houses slant toward the ground. n.* **1.** a point of view. *The news report took the slant that the actress had been treated unfairly.* **2.** a slanting direction or line. *He placed the ladder at a slant against the house.*

slo gan /slō′ gən/ *n.* **1.** a phrase or motto used by a particular group. *"Be prepared" is a Girl Scout slogan.* **2.** a phrase used to promote a product or service. *Advertisers try to create memorable slogans.*

sol i tar y /sol′ i ter′ ē/ *adj.* **1.** living or being alone. *The solitary traveler enjoyed being by himself.* **2.** single or sole. *There has not been a solitary instance of genius in our family.*

span /span/ *n.* **1.** a space of time. *My younger sister has an attention span of about five minutes.* **2.** the distance between two sections or supports. *The span of the Golden Gate Bridge is 1,280 meters. v.* **spans, spanning, spanned.** to extend across or over. *The Bay Bridge spans the San Francisco Bay.*

sparse /spärs/ *adj.* thinly spread; scattered. *The rural area had a very sparse population.*

spher i cal /sfer′ i kəl/ *adj.* shaped like a ball. *Globes have spherical shapes.*

stran ded /stran′ dəd/ *adj.* a form of **strand.** left in a helpless or difficult position. *Being stranded at sea has been the background for many adventure stories.*

stroll /strōl/ *v.* **strolls, strolling, strolled.** to walk unhurriedly. *They enjoyed strolling through the park on Sunday afternoons.*

suede /swād/ *n.* a soft, velvety leather. *My mother's jacket of green suede keeps her warm.*

sul len /sul′ ən/ *adj.* silent and gloomy. *The sullen child spent the afternoon in his room.*

su per flu ous /soo pûr′ floo əs/ *adj.* more than enough; more than is wanted or needed. *The amount of time Robert's relatives stayed at his house was superfluous.*

su pe ri or /sə pir′ ē ər/ *adj.* **1.** higher, better, or greater. *The food in this restaurant is superior to the dishes of other area eateries.* **2.** higher in status or rank. *A major is the superior officer of a captain.* **3.** haughty or proud. *A superior attitude wins few friends. n.* a person in a higher position. *The president of a company is the superior of the vice president.*

/a/	at
/ā/	late
/â/	care
/ä/	father
/e/	set
/ē/	me
/i/	it
/ī/	kite
/o/	ox
/ō/	rose
/ô/	brought
	raw
/oi/	coin
/oo/	book
/oo/	too
/or/	form
/ou/	out
/u/	up
/yoo/	cube
/ûr/	turn
	germ
	learn
	firm
	work
/ə/	about
	chicken
	pencil
	cannon
	circus
/ch/	chair
/hw/	which
/ng/	ring
/sh/	shop
/th/	thin
/ŧħ/	there
/zh/	treasure

su per sti tious /sōō´ pər stish´ əs/ *adj.* having or showing a belief based on ignorance and fear. *A superstitious person will not walk under a ladder.*

sym pa thize /sim´ pə thīz´/ *v.* **sympathizes, sympathizing, sympathized. 1.** to feel or express compassion. *I sympathized with my friend when she did not win the prize.* **2.** to agree with. *The townspeople sympathize with the mayor's efforts to reduce crime.*

sym pho ny /sim´ fə nē/ *n.* a long musical work written for an orchestra. *That symphony is a famous composition.*

symp tom /simp´ təm/ *n.* **1.** a sign of an illness. *A headache is a symptom of the flu.* **2.** a sign of something. *Drooping leaves on a plant are a symptom of drought.*

T

tab loid /tab´ loid/ *n.* a newspaper having pages smaller than an ordinary newspaper and that often publishes sensational stories. *Many tabloids contain articles about celebrities.*

tab u late /tab´ yə lāt´/ *v.* **tabulates, tabulating, tabulated.** to arrange in columns or lists. *Census bureaus tabulate information about the residents living in a country or region.*

tan gi ble /tan´ jə bəl/ *adj.* able to be touched. *Food and clothing are tangible objects.*

ta per /tā´ pər/ *v.* **tapers, tapering, tapered. 1.** to make or become gradually narrower. *The popular pants taper at the bottom.* **2.** to become less and less. *The snow tapered off by noon.*

tart /tärt/ *adj.* sour in taste; sharp, not sweet. *Green apples have a tart flavor. n.* a pastry shell with a filling. *Apricot tarts are my favorite.*

tat tered /tat´ ərd/ *adj.* a form of **tatter.** torn in shreds or hanging. *I finally had to throw away my favorite shirt when it became too tattered to wear.*

temp ta tion /temp tā´ shən/ *n.* **1.** attraction; the act of tempting or luring. *The temptation of the food dropped on the floor was too great for the dog to resist.* **2.** something that tempts. *Chocolate cake is a temptation that is hard for many people to resist.*

ten ta tive /ten´ tə tiv/ *adj.* not decided; uncertain. *We made tentative plans to go hiking Saturday morning.*

ter mi nate /tûr´ mə nāt´/ *v.* **terminates, terminating, terminated.** to bring or come to an end. *The brook terminates at this point in the trail.*

tor rent /tor´ ənt/ *n.* **1.** a violent stream or downpour. *The flood brought torrents of water over the low-lying lands.* **2.** a violent flow of anything. *The student brought a torrent of criticism on himself when he insulted the teacher.*

tox ic /tok´ sik/ *adj.* poisonous. *It is illegal for factories to dump toxic waste into bodies of water.*

tril o gy /tril´ ə jē/ *n.* a series of three closely related works. *The author's three novels make up a famous trilogy.*

tri mes ter /trī´ mes tər/ *n.* a period of three months. *A year can be divided into four trimesters.*

tri um phant /trī um´ fənt/ *adj.* successful or victorious. *The champion was triumphant in three straight matches.*

truce /trōōs/ *n.* a temporary halt to fighting. *A truce must be agreed to by both sides.*

trudge /truj/ *v.* **trudges, trudging, trudged.** to walk slowly and wearily. *They trudged back home after being lost for an hour in the woods.*

tur bu lent /tûr´ byə lənt/ *adj.* agitated; of or causing disorder. *The U.S. Civil War was a turbulent period of history.*

twine /twīn/ *v.* **twines, twining, twined.** to twist or coil one thing around another. *The children twined ribbons around the pole. n.* a strong string made of two or more strands twisted together. *We wrapped all our packages with twine and loaded them into the car.*

ty rant /tī′ rənt/ *n.* **1.** a person who uses power in a cruel or unjust manner. *The company president was a tyrant who was disliked by his employees.* **2.** a person who has absolute power and rules in a cruel way. *The dictator was a tyrant who became rich at the expense of the people living in the country.*

U

un der go /un′ dər gō′/ *v.* **undergoes, undergoing, underwent.** to experience; to go through. *Our car is undergoing repairs in the shop.*

u ni son /yōō′ nə sən/ *n.* **1.** making the same sounds or movements at the same time. *The children recited the nursery rhyme in unison.* **2.** sameness in pitch. *The second sopranos and the altos sang the song in unison.*

un kempt /un kempt′/ *adj.* not groomed or combed. *Some teenagers think unkempt hair is fashionable.*

un pre dic ta ble /un′ pri dik′ tə bəl/ *adj.* not certain. *The weather often is unpredictable.*

un re lent ing /un′ ri len′ ting/ *adj.* harsh, unchanging. *My uncle can be unrelenting in his criticism of city government.*

V

val iant /val′ yənt/ *adj.* brave or courageous. *Our team made a valiant effort to win the last game of the season.*

van dal ism /van′ də liz′ əm/ *n.* purposeful, unlawful destruction. *The vandalism of their parade float saddened all the students.*

ven om ous /ven′ ə məs/ *adj.* **1.** poisonous. *About one-fifth of snake species are venomous.* **2.** malicious or spiteful. *Her venomous remark earned her no friends.*

ver dict /vûr′ dikt/ *n.* **1.** the decision of a jury in a trial. *The jury returned a unanimous verdict of "guilty."* **2.** a decision or conclusion. *The children's verdict is in—the book is the best on the reading list.*

ver i fy /ver′ ə fī/ *v.* **verifies, verifying, verified. 1.** to confirm; to prove to be true. *My father verified the time of the plane's arrival by calling the airline.* **2.** to check or test the accuracy of. *Scientists verify the results of their experiments by performing additional tests.*

ve to /vē′ tō/ *v.* **vetoing, vetoed.** to reject a bill passed by a lawmaking body. *Some members of Congress knew that the president would veto the bill.* *n., pl.* **vetoes.** the power of a president, governor, or other executive to keep an act from taking effect. *That politician holds the record for total number of vetoes used during a presidency.*

vi tal /vī′ təl/ *adj.* **1.** relating to life. *The vital organs of the human body include the heart and the lungs.* **2.** necessary; of great importance. *A good map is vital for our wilderness trip.*

/a/	at
/ā/	late
/â/	care
/ä/	father
/e/	set
/ē/	me
/i/	it
/ī/	kite
/o/	ox
/ō/	rose
/ô/	brought
	raw
/oi/	coin
/o͝o/	book
/o͞o/	too
/or/	form
/ou/	out
/u/	up
/yo͞o/	cube
/ûr/	turn
	germ
	learn
	firm
	work
/ə/	about
	chicken
	pencil
	cannon
	circus
/ch/	chair
/hw/	which
/ng/	ring
/sh/	shop
/th/	thin
/th̶/	there
/zh/	treasure

W

wel fare /wel′ fâr/ *n.* **1.** the condition of being happy and healthy; well-being. *Parents are always concerned about the welfare of their children.* **2.** money or other aid given by the government to people in need. *That proposal suggests adding life-skills and work-training programs to the system of welfare.*

whim /hwim/ *n.* a sudden or unexpected idea or desire. *We went to the high school baseball game on a whim.*

wrath /rath/ *n.* extreme anger. *Legendary outlaw Robin Hood provoked the wrath of King John.*

A—F Word Bank

G—M Word Bank

N—S Word Bank

T—Z Word Bank